# Book of Harmony

chapter 1 + 2          9/15 class

# Book of Harmony

Spirit and Service in the *Lutheran Confessions*

Martin J. Lohrmann

Fortress Press
*Minneapolis*

BOOK OF HARMONY

Spirit and Service in the *Lutheran Confessions*

Cover image: Thinkstock © 2016: Martin Luther and Philip Melancthon

Cover design: Alisha Lofgren

*Library of Congress Cataloging-in-Publication Data*

Print ISBN: 978-1-5064-0018-1

eBook ISBN: 978-1-5064-0110-2

The paper used in this publication meets the minimum requirements of American National Standard for Information Sciences — Permanence of Paper for Printed Library Materials, ANSI Z329.48-1984.

Manufactured in the U.S.A.

This book was produced using Pressbooks.com, and PDF rendering was done by PrinceXML.

# Contents

# Acknowledgements

This project builds upon research and experience I have gathered as a parish pastor, church history teacher, and student of Reformation history. As pastor of Christ Ascension Lutheran Church in Philadelphia, PA, I enjoyed sharing the Lutheran tradition with congregation members who were new to this particular branch of Christianity and those who had been longtime learners within it. While in Philadelphia, I also benefited from the wisdom and comradery of great colleagues, including fellow Lutherans, my ecumenical Bible study group, and friends in the interfaith community. Their insights and encouragement stayed with me as I wrote this book, even though I now live almost a thousand miles away. I also continue to learn from the great teaching and scholarship of my PhD advisor, Timothy Wengert.

I have been fortunate to develop these ideas with a variety of audiences, especially students at Wartburg Theological Seminary in Dubuque, Iowa and with participants of the Luther Academy of the Rockies near Estes Park, Colorado (summer 2015). Also, my colleague Troy Troftgruben started an ecumenical, cross-disciplinary writing group among newish theology professors in Dubuque when I was starting this book; these colleagues read the earliest draft of the first chapters and gave great feedback. I also received helpful ideas from several of my family members and from my research assistant Matthew Seegert. Michael Gibson of Fortress Press has overseen this book from proposal to publication; Layne Meyer has served as project manager. My thanks go to all of you. I would also like to share my appreciation for the blessing of so many wonderful teachers, colleagues, mentors and friends over the years, whose concerns for the relationship between faith, knowledge, and life together have shaped how I approach theology. As Martin Luther wrote (paraphrasing Aristotle) in his *Large Catechism*, "God, parents, and teachers can never be sufficiently thanked or repaid."[1]

I am very grateful for my colleagues at Wartburg Theological Seminary, who deeply care about cultivating and being a community "where learning leads to mission and mission informs learning." I am especially thankful for the work of emeritus professor Ralph Quere (my Lutheran Confessions teacher) and President Louise Johnson, who values the richness of the past while leading us into the challenges and opportunities of sharing the faith in the early twenty-first century.

Finally: I want to thank my great friend Brian for letting me share the story that begins this book and for being a truly great friend for a lifetime; and I thank my wife Carrie and our children—Hilde, Jonah, and Theodore—for sharing so much love and support as a family.

I dedicate this book to all readers with the verse Matt 5:16. It is a passage from the Sermon on the Mount that is part of the baptismal liturgy and a saying that my Grandma Thelma often used to bless and encourage those around her: "Let your light so shine before others, so that they may see your good works and give glory to your Father in heaven."

Martin J. Lohrmann
Dubuque, Iowa
Reformation Sunday, 2015

1. BC 404.130.

# Abbreviations

Ap      *Apology of the Augsburg Confession*, in *The Book of Concord: The Confessions of the Evangelical Lutheran Church*. Edited by Robert Kolb and Timothy J. Wengert. Minneapolis: Fortress, 2000.

Arand, Kolb, and Nestingen      *The Lutheran Confessions: History and Theology of the Book of Concord*. By Charles P. Arand, Robert Kolb, and James A. Nestingen. Minneapolis: Fortress, 2012.

BC      *The Book of Concord: The Confessions of the Evangelical Lutheran Church*. Edited by Robert Kolb and Timothy J. Wengert. Minneapolis: Fortress, 2000.

CA      *The Augsburg Confession*, in *The Book of Concord: The Confessions of the Evangelical Lutheran Church*. Edited by Robert Kolb and Timothy J. Wengert. Minneapolis: Fortress, 2000.

Ep      *Epitome of the Formula of Concord*, in *The Book of Concord: The Confessions of the Evangelical Lutheran Church*. Edited by Robert Kolb and Timothy J. Wengert. Minneapolis: Fortress, 2000.

LC      *The Large Catechism*, in *The Book of Concord: The Confessions of the Evangelical Lutheran Church. Edited by Robert Kolb and Timothy J. Wengert. Minneapolis: Fortress, 2000.*

LW      Martin Luther. *Luther's Works*. American edition. 55 volumes. Philadelphia: Fortress; St. Louis: Concordia, 1955-86.

PL      *Patrologia cursus completus. Series Latina*. 221 volumes. Paris & Turnout, 1859-1866.

SA      *The Smalcald Articles*, in *The Book of Concord: The Confessions of the Evangelical Lutheran Church*. Edited by Robert Kolb and Timothy J. Wengert. Minneapolis: Fortress, 2000.

SC      *The Small Catechism*, in *The Book of Concord: The Confessions of the Evangelical Lutheran Church*. Edited by Robert Kolb and Timothy J. Wengert. Minneapolis: Fortress, 2000.

SD      *Solid Declaration of the Formula of Concord*, in *The Book of Concord: The Confessions of the Evangelical Lutheran Church.* Edited by Robert Kolb and Timothy J. Wengert. Minneapolis: Fortress, 2000.

Tr      Treatise on the Power and Primacy of the Pope, in *The Book of Concord: The Confessions of the Evangelical Lutheran Church.* Edited by Robert Kolb and Timothy J. Wengert. Minneapolis: Fortress, 2000.

WA      Martin Luther. *Luthers Werke: Kritische Gesamtausgabe.* [*Schriften.*] 65 volumes. Weimar: Böhlau, 1883-1993.

# Preface

I became a student of Christian history at an early age. One weekend when we were about twelve years old, my best friend Brian stayed at my house while his parents went out of town. That Sunday, Brian—who grew up attending his local Roman Catholic parish—came with us to church in our Lutheran congregation. It happened to be Reformation Sunday, the last Sunday of October when Lutherans observe the Reformation that started with the appearance, on October 31, 1517, of Martin Luther's *95 Theses* on indulgences.

Having grown up Lutheran, it seemed like just another Reformation Sunday to me: remembering Martin Luther and giving thanks for his reforming ministry. To my Catholic friend, however, it was a scandal. "What was that all about?!" Brian fumed as we left church. "What was so terrible about Catholics that you guys had to throw 95 feces at our church doors?!"

After explaining the difference between theses and feces, I realized that I needed to learn more for myself about the Reformation and my Lutheran tradition. I wanted to know why a story I grew up cherishing could be so shocking to my best friend. I started to check out books about Luther from local libraries, read whatever I could find about the Reformation at church, school or home, and paid careful attention to religious conversations whenever they came up. I continued to study these themes in college, with majors in history and humanities and a minor in theology. My decision to pursue a career in Lutheran ministry also included a desire to learn more about my Lutheran heritage so that I could interpret it in meaningful ways both for Lutherans and for people of other religious backgrounds. As I learned from Brian, a good starting place for those conversations comes from explaining the meaning of unusual words, like "theses," which can easily be mistaken for something else; in Luther's time, theses were points raised for the sake of discussion and teaching.

Of course, Brian had not simply misheard a new vocabulary word on that Reformation Sunday. He was right to think that the way the Reformation had been presented in my congregation had included putting down Roman Catholicism. He found himself on the receiving end of the powerful but faulty logic that asserts: since I know my religious tradition to be true and life-giving, then other traditions must be false and misleading to the degree that they differ from mine. Part of my own journey has included wrestling with the question of how members of faith traditions can balance commitment to their own religious heritage with respect for the commitments of others. While my interest in this topic started with a personal experience, it also now comes with a broader concern to cultivate the kinds of positive interpersonal and communal relationships that build people up rather than tear them down.

As easy as it is to slip into self-centered ways of thinking, the Golden Rule of Matt 7:12 provides a great corrective. Jesus said, "In everything do to others as you would have them do to you." Applying the Golden Rule to my work as a Reformation historian and Lutheran Christian means that I hope to share some of the insights about God, the Bible, faith, and daily life that I have learned from the Lutheran tradition. I have personally found that Lutheranism offers rich ideas for today, especially in the consistent focus on how faith in Jesus Christ fills and re-forms everyday life with grace. As I first experienced on that Reformation Sunday with Brian years ago, however, my appreciation of this tradition should not come at the expense of others. Therefore, as I share insights from the Lutheran tradition in this book, I aim to do so in ways that honor the histories, views and experiences of neighbors in this diverse world. Simple as it may seem, the Golden Rule provides a profound starting point both for claiming what is important to oneself and respecting others.

Even so, some readers may wonder why bother with Reformation history or with specific religious commitments? Aren't the conflicts of the past best left behind? Not necessarily. Rather than ignore differences in history and outlook, the Golden Rule suggests a far more interesting way to affirm both individuality and mutuality: taking time to notice uniqueness can open doors of acceptance rather than close them. When I think of myself as a boy, I remember wondering if my religious faith was something that would make my world bigger or smaller. Would my faith separate me from the people around me or encourage me to live well with others whose backgrounds differed from mine? Over the decades, I have discovered that learning about and living out my religious tradition has indeed opened new paths into a big and beautiful world, including learning from the people around me.

## What This Book Is About

In 1580, Reformation-era documents central to Lutheran preaching, teaching, and church life were brought together in a collection called the *Book of Concord*, which is full of thought-provoking theology and fascinating historical contexts. While this study will cover those theological and historical aspects, it will also show that the *Book of Concord* is filled with a basic spiritual concern that people's lives be rich in meaning and in service.

More than just a source of dusty dogmas or a relic of history, the *Book of Concord* offers valuable insights for people today. As a spiritual resource, its pages passionately describe things like faith in God, care for human souls, and Holy Spirit-filled ways to live. As a practical guide, it offers concrete ways for people to live out their faith amid the complexities of the real world.

While this focus on Spirit and service may sound simple enough, a historical and theological irony has accompanied the *Book of Concord* from its outset: this work that aimed to serve as a platform for spiritual harmony also contributed to the separation of Lutherans from Roman Catholic communities and from other branches of Protestantism. On that Reformation Sunday with Brian, for instance, centuries of division between Protestants and Roman Catholics became very real for us in our hometown of Walla Walla, Washington, far from the Lutheran Saxony or Catholic Rome of the 1500s. Such divisions have direct roots in Reformation-era writings like the *Book of Concord*.

Are divisions like these permanently built into the faith traditions people carry with them? Or—as in the discussion of the Golden Rule above—might mutually edifying encounters come when we respectfully address challenging points of difference and particularity? This study offers the view that the *Book of Concord*'s care for truth and service reveals the great extent to which the Lutheran reformers valued lives of faith, hope, and love more than their own partisan desire to be right; they offered an expansive rather than reductive vision of human life in a complex world. I would even like to suggest that we in the early twenty-first century have opportunities to live into their hopes for harmony in ways that people in previous times could hardly have imagined.

With a focus on the Holy Spirit and Christian service in the *Book of Concord*, this study will identify core characteristics of the Lutheran tradition, including some traits that Lutherans share in common with other Christians and some that remain distinctive. For a variety of historical and theological reasons, Lutherans occupy a strange place in the history of Christianity. Although obviously identified with the beginning of Protestant Christianity, Lutherans represent a relatively small portion of Protestants today. In very broad numbers, if there are about eight hundred million Protestants in the world, just under ten percent of them (around seventy million) are Lutheran. Thus, even though Lutherans have played an important role in Christian history, they represent a distinctive and frequently unfamiliar branch of global Christianity. This book will aid readers' general familiarity with the Lutheran tradition.

As a work of "public theology," this book aims to interpret the *Book of Concord* in ways that both Lutherans and those outside the tradition might find enriching.[1] I hope that Lutheran readers will gain new or renewed appreciation for their tradition and that readers who may be less familiar with Lutheranism will learn some of the values and principles of this nearly five-hundred-year-old branch of Christianity. While I highly recommend that people read the documents in the *Book of Concord* for themselves sometime, this book does not assume or require familiarity with those sources.

## Conversations between the Past and the Present

What does it mean to learn from the past? On one hand, the past can seem to stand above contemporary questions and experiences, as if to say: the way it was then is the way things ought to be now. While the stability of such a view can be reassuring, it can also impose past norms on the present in unhelpful ways. On the other hand, we may be tempted to think that people in the past were so different that we have nothing to learn from them; or perhaps we suppose that the past only contained the kinds of prejudices and ignorance that enlightened modern people need to leave behind. This study navigates these extremes, first by acknowledging that we can learn much from those who came before us, and second, by expecting that contemporary viewpoints will build upon the witness and wisdom of the past in inspiring ways.

For example, when revising his excellent 1984 two-volume study of Christian history for the 2010s, Justo González asked an important question: Why update history? In response, he described "the fascinating dialogue between the present and the past that is the very essence of history: a dialogue in which the past addresses us, but does so in terms of our present questions."[2] Although it may sometimes

---

1. Jeffrey Stout, *Democracy and Tradition* (Princeton: Princeton, 2004), 112: "The vocation of theologians . . . is to make explicit the commitments implicit in a community's practices as an aid to reflective self-understanding. But their contribution to discourse outside of the church consists in a kind of thick description that allows fellow citizens to correct prejudice and misunderstanding concerning what believers think and care about." See also page 113: "If you express theological commitments in a reflective and sustained way, while addressing fellow citizens as citizens, you are 'doing theology' publicly—and in that sense doing public theology."

seem as if history is settled, the past speaks to us in new ways as we approach it from different perspectives. In this study, it is not that the *Book of Concord* has changed, but that we in the twenty-first century have new questions to ask it and new insights to harvest from it.

This lively interaction between old and new has been built into both the Christian tradition and the Lutheran Reformation. While I mentioned the Golden Rule above, another passage from the Gospel of Matthew similarly informs the study of history: Jesus said, "every scribe trained for the kingdom of heaven is like the master of a household who brings out of his treasure what is new and what is old" (Matt 13:52). With this saying, Jesus invited people to see a life of faith as a continuous adventure of setting new treasures alongside old ones in fascinating and enriching ways.

A contemporary example of how past and present mutually enrich each other comes from the rock band U2. While preparing for another tour after decades of performing, the singer Bono explained how the band's efforts to balance the old and new would be the "dialectic of this tour."[3] That is, the band hoped to bring out the best of their old material and set it alongside its newer work to create an inspiring concert experience.

In a wonderful coincidence, Bono's word "dialectic" is a key word within Lutheran theology. It refers to the learning that happens through dialogue with others. The Greek philosopher Socrates provided classic examples of dialectical thinking, as he guided people to new learning through conversation. In Plato's dialogue *Meno*, for instance, Socrates taught basic principles of geometry to an uneducated boy, making sure that the boy came to all of the conclusions by himself as they worked on problems together.[4]

In a similar way, the Lutheran reformers of the 1500s valued dialectic as a tool for combining the wisdom of the past with the needs of the present. They taught people core concepts from the Bible and the

2. Justo González, *The Story of Christianity, Volume 1: The Early Church to the Dawn of the Reformation*, revised and updated (New York: HarperCollins, 2010), xvi.
3. Andy Greene, "Inside U2's 'Innocence' Spectacle," *Rolling Stone* issue 1236 (June 4, 2015), 33.
4. Plato, *Great Dialogues of Plato*, translated by W.H.D. Rouse (New York: Penguin, 1984), 43–49.

Christian tradition, with the understanding that people and situations inevitably change across time and place. Rather than leaving their successors with a rigid theological system or a fixed set of answers that only fit their era, worldview or culture, the Lutheran reformers used dialectical thinking to provide a firm set of principles that could be meaningfully translated across a variety of settings. They aimed to identify clear central points around which all kinds of adaptation and uniqueness could exist in harmony.

With the understanding that the Lutheran reformers were aware of difference in situations and customs, it is fair to say that dialectic and change were built into the tradition. As the book proceeds, I hope to describe this tradition in such a way that "most Lutherans, most of the time" would agree with my interpretation. I expect that some Lutherans will not agree with everything I write here, which is itself a noteworthy side of the Lutheran experience. What does it mean for a community to embrace its internal diversity and to trust that harmony can exist alongside difference? This has been an important and lively theme among Lutherans since early in the Reformation.

Finally, this book contains the critical awareness that Lutheranism spans the globe and is not the cultural possession of certain European or North American groups. Themselves aware of 1500 years of diverse Christian witness, the Lutheran reformers fully expected that people would continue to have different ways of thinking about and living out the gospel message that God justifies the ungodly "as a gift on account of Christ through faith."[5] They knew that unity has long existed alongside diverse ways of being Christian. Our unique global perspectives in the early twenty-first century provide compelling reasons to revisit the past with fresh eyes. With so many pressing challenges in our closely-connected yet highly-fragmented world, ideas like concord, harmony, spirit and service are as important as ever.

We are all on a journey in life, individually and together. Learning

---

5. CA IV 39.1–41.2. The description of God "who justifies the ungodly" is from Rom 4:5.

from those who came before us offers a great way to enrich the experience, widen the conversation, and grow in knowledge and love.

# 1

---

# Introduction to the *Book of Concord*

## What Is the *Book of Concord*?

From the Latin "with heart," concord means harmony and peace. The
*Book of Concord* (*Concordia* in Latin) is the collection of writings from
the 1500s that many Lutherans have long used as the biblically-based
foundation of their Christian faith and practice. As a title, *Concordia*
expresses the great hope of unity in faith and service that many
religious communities share and strive for. Also, uniqueness and
diversity are built into this idea of harmony, because it is impossible to
be harmonious if everyone is singing the same note.

As a collection of writings rather than a single work, the *Book of
Concord* has multiple authors. Additionally, even if individual sections
carry the name of one person, all the works grew out of a highly
collegial environment, in which reformers discussed their work with
each other before publication. Even more, theologians and politicians
outside the writing circle frequently added their signatures to the
documents to show their public support for these texts. Seen in this
light, all the works within the *Book of Concord* belong to communities
rather than individuals. Of the individuals who contributed to the

writing of these texts, the most prominent and frequent authors are Martin Luther and Philip Melanchthon. For this reason, it is helpful to get acquainted with these two reformers.

Born in 1483, Luther entered an Observant Augustinian monastery in 1505. The "observant" part of that name came from the seriousness with which these monks took their religious callings. The "Augustinian" part derives from the fact that this medieval monastic order looked back to St. Augustine (354–430), a North African bishop whose theology emphasized the amazing grace of God who justifies the ungodly.[1] Encouraged by his superiors in the order to continue his studies, Luther earned a doctorate and became a theology professor at the University of Wittenberg in 1512. The publication of his 95 Theses in 1517 led to a movement for reform of the church in Europe and the beginning of Protestant Christianity.[2]

Though about thirteen years younger than Luther, Philip Melanchthon became a valued colleague in Wittenberg as soon as he began teaching there in 1518. Especially gifted in Greek and Latin, Melanchthon taught his students the classical subjects of grammar, rhetoric and logic in order to understand and share Christian faith and human wisdom as clearly as possible. During a career that spanned more than fifty years in Wittenberg, Melanchthon taught nearly every subject at the university. His interest in teaching the building blocks of faith and fundamental educational concepts meant that he was not interested in being ordained or receiving a doctorate (even though he wrote the exams for PhD students!).[3] His keen mind and effective

---

1. As mentioned above, the phrase God "who justifies the ungodly" comes from Rom 4:5. This verse was an important part of Augustine's theology in works like On the Trinity and On the Spirit and the Letter; see Augustine, Later Works, edited and translated by John Burnaby, Library of Christian Classics, Vol. 8 (Philadelphia: Westminster, 1955), 114, 201, 205, 238, 240, and 244; the Latin citation from On the Trinity occurs in PL 42:1048.
2. Biographies of Martin Luther in English include Martin Brecht, Martin Luther, 3 volumes, translated by James Schaaf (Philadelphia and Minneapolis: Fortress, 1985–1993); James Kittelson, Luther the Reformer: The Story of the Man and His Career (Minneapolis: Augsburg, 1986); Martin Marty, Martin Luther (New York: Penguin, 2004); and Heiko Oberman, Luther: Man between God and the Devil, translated by Eileen Walliser-Schwarzbart (New Haven, CT: Yale, 1989).
3. Heinz Scheible, "Fifty Years of Melanchthon Research," Lutheran Quarterly 26, 2 (Summer 2012): 168.

reforms of church, society and schools justly earned him the title *Praeceptor Germania*—teacher of Germany.[4]

After Luther died in 1546, religious and political controversies hounded the Lutheran movement, with external critiques coming from both the Roman Catholic side and from other Protestant communities led by reformers like Huldrych Zwingli and John Calvin. Among themselves, Lutherans also started to disagree about essential points of faith and practice, making it difficult for leaders and congregations to build up the church together. Concord seemed far away.

In 1577, a second generation of church leaders put together a statement called the *Formula of Concord* that addressed key disputed points. In 1580, theologians and politicians hoping to further resolve these disputes combined the *Formula* with writings by Luther and Melanchthon to create the *Book of Concord*. By accepting these works as clear statements of their shared faith, leaders of church and society wanted to put days of *discord* behind them.

More than two-thirds of German Lutheran lands gave their approval to the *Book of Concord* at that time.[5] This partial acceptance reveals both success and failure in attaining religious harmony. On the negative side, some parties rejected the *Book of Concord* out of the conviction that their concerns had been misrepresented or gone unheard. In the centuries that followed the Reformation, disputes between Orthodox Lutherans who emphasized "right doctrine" and Lutheran Pietists who stressed "right practice" might suggest another failure to achieve lasting concord.[6] Further, the frequently contentious history of Lutheranism's spread beyond Europe shows how hard it has sometimes been for Lutherans to agree on essential points of belief and practice.[7]

---

4. Recent articles on Melanchthon in English can be found in *Philip Melanchthon: Then and Now (1497-1997)* (Columbia, SC: Lutheran Theological Southern Seminary, 1999) and Timothy Wengert, *Philip Melanchthon, Speaker of the Reformation: Wittenberg's Other Reformer* (Burlington, VT: Ashgate, 2010).

5. Charles P. Arand, Robert Kolb and James Nestingen, *The Lutheran Confessions: History and Theology of The Book of Concord* (Minneapolis: Fortress Press, 2012), 277.

6. Eric Gritsch, *A History of Lutheranism* (Minneapolis: Fortress, 2002), chapters 4 and 5.

7. Mark Granquist, *Lutherans in America: A New History* (Minneapolis: Fortress, 2015), especially chapter 6. On global Lutheranism, see Jan Pranger, "Lutherans in the World Church," J. Paul Rajashekar, "Lutheranism in Asia and the Indian Subcontinent," and Munib Younan, "The Future of the Lutheran Reformation Tradition: From the Perspective of Palestinian Christians," in *The*

Despite all this, the *Book of Concord* succeeded in many of its original goals. First, it demonstrated that Lutherans value decision-making that comes by consensus and not by coercion, even if that means that some will go their own ways. Second, the *Book of Concord* did cultivate unity among many people in the sixteenth century. Original signers included three electors of the Holy Roman Empire (powerful German princes with the right to elect the emperor), eighty other heads of state (nobility and city councils), and more than eight thousand pastors and theologians. Those who adopted the *Book of Concord* lived across a geographical area that ranged from Prussia on the Baltic Sea to Württemberg near France and Switzerland.

Though Scandinavian Lutherans did not adopt all the writings within the *Book of Concord* as normative for their churches, they shared with the Germans a common focus on the *Augsburg Confession* and Luther's *Small Catechism* as definitive expressions of their churches' teaching and worship life. The two largest Lutheran church bodies in the United States—the Evangelical Lutheran Church in America (ELCA) and The Lutheran Church—Missouri Synod (LCMS)—both affirm all the writings within the *Book of Concord* as normative, though the ELCA prioritizes the *Augsburg Confession* as the basis for unity in the gospel.[8]

An important example of Lutheranism adapting in a non-European setting comes from the Protestant Christian Batak Church. This Indonesian church body belongs to the international Lutheran World Federation to which a majority of the world's Lutheran churches belong. Recognizing the great historical distance between sixteenth-century Germany and twentieth-century Indonesia, the Batak Church affirmed its Lutheran heritage and the teachings of the *Augsburg Confession* while also writing its own foundational confessional statement.[9] The Batak Church provides a good example of how the

*Future of Lutheranism in a Global Context*, edited by Arland Jacobson and James Aageson (Minneapolis: Augsburg Fortress, 2008).

8. "Model Constitution for Congregations of the Evangelical Lutheran Church in America, 2013," http://www.elca.org/Resources/Office-of-the-Secretary, section C2.05. And "Constitution, Bylaws, and Articles of Incorporation," The Lutheran Church—Missouri Synod (Kirkwood, MO: 2010), 13.

9. Rajashekar, 71.

Lutheran tradition possesses a flexible foundation for Christian unity amid difference.

## Evangelical Lutheran Confessions: What's in a Name?

The first editions of the *Book of Concord* were published in Dresden, Saxony in 1580 [title page below, left].[10] English translations have been available in the United States since the mid-1800s, with the latest English-language edition published in 2000 [cover image, below right]. It was edited jointly by Robert Kolb and Timothy Wengert, Reformation scholars who belong to two different branches of American Lutheranism.

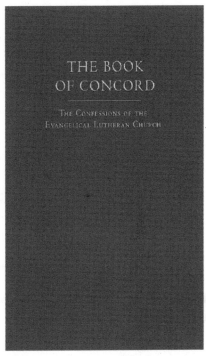

The 1580 edition begins with the book's title in all caps—*CONCORDIA*—followed by the Hebrew letters that spell the unpronounceable name of God, YHWH, as an invocation of and

10. Image is in the public domain.

dedication to the Lord whose mysterious name is I AM WHO I AM (Exod 3:14).

The cover of the English-language edition includes a short subtitle, *The Confessions of the Evangelical Lutheran Church*. This subtitle is an adaptation of the German title page, which in English begins: "Christian, Recapitulated, Unanimous Confession of the Teaching and Faith by the Undersigned Electors, Princes, and Estates of the *Augsburg Confession* and Their Theologians."[11]

From this subtitle, the contents of the *Book of Concord* are often called the "Lutheran Confessions." As a summary of its contents, the name "Lutheran Confessions" offers the benefit of brevity, though further explanation is probably needed. First, what kind of "confessions" are Lutherans talking about? Second, what is the "Evangelical Lutheran Church" that holds to such confessions?

First, on confession. In everyday usage, a confession means an admission of guilt. Since the time of the early church, Christians have used this word to describe the acknowledgement of sins or wrongs committed against God and other people. The Christian practice of repentance has long included either the public or private confession of sin as part of the ritual of reconciliation.

In a similar sense, St. Augustine's classical work *Confessions* (written around the year 400) was an early "tell-all" autobiography of how a proud, self-absorbed scholar unexpectedly became a servant of God and the church. It presents a confession of his past sins, as well as a confession (or profession) of his faith in Jesus Christ, as he expressed in the prayer to God that opens the book: "You stir [us] to take pleasure in praising you, because you have made us for yourself, and our heart is restless until it rests in you."[12]

This second sense of confession as a profession of faith in God is what Lutherans mean when they speak of their "confessional writings." Beyond Augustine's *Confessions*, for instance, this usage became more common as Christians in Western Europe started to introduce creeds

---

11. BC 3, with footnote 1, which explains the word recapitulation as "a technical term . . . for an exposition and reaffirmation of an earlier confession of faith."
12. Augustine, *Confessions*, translated by Henry Chadwick (Oxford: Oxford University Press, 1991), 3.

and other statements of belief with the words "we believe and confess" (*credimus et confitemur*). In this way, "confessing the faith" meant announcing personal and communal beliefs publicly.[13]

When Lutherans were asked to explain their beliefs and reforms to Holy Roman Emperor Charles V at the imperial congress (also called a "diet") held in the German city of Augsburg in 1530, the task of writing this new statement of faith primarily fell to Philip Melanchthon. He originally planned to describe this collective statement of Lutheran faith as an *apologia*, or defense. As he prepared the text, however, he realized that the situation required more than just an intellectual or theological defense of Reformation ideas. Spiritual and physical matters of life and death were at stake: spiritual, because of the seriousness with which the Lutherans took their understanding of gospel salvation and relationship with God; physical, because Emperor Charles could have tried to end the Reformation movement by force at any given moment. In fact, violence had already threatened to erupt in Augsburg in the first days of that diet.[14]

With these life-and-death realities in mind, Melanchthon gave his work the heading: "The Augsburg Confession. Confession of Faith by Certain Princes and Cities Presented to His Imperial Majesty in Augsburg in the year 1530."[15] Because Melanchthon presented Lutheran theology and reforms in this way, some scholars have suggested that he invented a new genre of Christian literature with the *Augsburg Confession*: the communal confession of faith.[16]

Luther had made a similar personal statement in his 1528 *Confession Concerning Christ's Supper*, as he clarified his beliefs so that no one would misunderstand them after he died (he had been gravely ill in 1527).[17] Melanchthon's work, however, presented the faith of an entire group as a shared confession. The physical danger that Charles' power posed to the reformers, to the political leaders of reforming lands, and to the

---

13. Arand, Kolb and Nestingen, 4.
14. Arand, Kolb and Nestingen, 104.
15. BC 30. Note: the title appears in the first published edition, May 1531.
16. Arand, Kolb, and Nestingen, 4.
17. LW 37:360–72.

common people themselves underscored the conviction and courage required to make this "confession" of the faith in Augsburg. For the Lutherans, confessing the faith was not only an intellectual exercise; it was an existential and spiritual event, as well.[18]

Given this background about what Lutherans mean by "confession" and confessional writings, we move to the Lutheran use of the word "evangelical." Evangelical comes from the Greek word *euangelion*, which means gospel or good news, as in the opening words of the Gospel of Mark: "The beginning of the good news [*euangelion*] of Jesus Christ, the Son of God" (1:1).

More than just being books in the genre of "gospels," the Lutherans identified the gospel with the singular message that God gives sinners grace, reconciliation and new life through faith in Christ. As Paul wrote in Rom 1:16, the gospel "is the power of God for salvation to everyone who has faith."[19] Emphasizing the centrality of this message, the Lutheran Confessions assert that "the chief worship of God is to preach the gospel."[20] While Christianity and church life can include any number of spiritual and practical aspects, for Lutherans the sharing and receiving of this particular message of good news always comes first. This is the sense in which Lutherans have long used the word "evangelical" to describe their theology. As Luther wrote in his *Brief Instruction on What to Look for and Expect in the Gospels* (1521), "The gospel is a story about Christ, God's and David's Son, who died and was raised and is established as Lord."[21]

It is worth noting that in English "evangelical" came to be associated with the Great Awakenings of the 1700s and 1800s, characterized by charismatic preaching and an emphasis on personal conversion. While

18. Robert Kolb, *Confessing the Faith: Reformers Define the Church, 1530-1580* (St. Louis: Concordia, 1991), 13–42.
19. SD 582.3-6. See also Luther's *A Brief Instruction on What to Look for and Expect in the Gospels*, LW 35:117–24, and his Preface to the New Testament, LW 35:360. In the 1521 *Loci Communes* (as well as many other places), Melanchthon followed Rom 1:17 in defining gospel as "the promise of the grace and mercy of God, especially the forgiveness of sins and the testimony of God's goodwill toward us;" Philip Melanchthon, "Loci Communes Theologici," *Melanchthon and Bucer*, edited by Wilhelm Pauck and translated by Lowell J. Satre (Philadelphia: Westminster, 1969), 71.
20. Ap 229.42.
21. LW 35:118.

Lutherans care deeply about good gospel preaching and a personal relationship with God, there is enough of a difference between these traditions that the application of "evangelical" to both groups may be misleading. For instance, where American Evangelicalism emphasizes that people need to make a personal choice for Christ, Lutheranism emphasizes that conversion is the work of the Holy Spirit through baptism and the word of God, a lifelong relationship that has its beginning, growth and culmination in God.[22] When it appears in this work, "evangelical" will be used in the sixteenth-century sense as a description of reforms based upon the gospel teaching that Luther emphasized.

Like many labels, the name "Lutheran" was originally used as an insult. Luther's longtime theological adversary Johann Eck first put the word "Lutheran" in print, as he meant it to be a disparaging description of a heretical sect.[23] For several reasons, Luther himself did not like the name. Instead, in a 1522 tract he expressed his hope that the reform movement around him could be known as just plain "Christian" rather than Lutheran.[24] Later he came to prefer the name "evangelical," a word connecting church reforms to the gospel[25] and an adjective that Luther had been using since at least 1517 to describe his work.[26] This usage remains common in German, in which the name *Evangelisch* can refer to Protestants in general or Lutherans in particular.

When not calling themselves evangelicals, Lutherans in the sixteenth century described themselves as people and churches of the *Augsburg Confession*, as seen above on the title page of the 1580 *Book of Concord*. This description is still used among several Lutheran church bodies, especially those in central European countries like Austria,

---

22. On the emergence of a general "evangelical consensus" in the United States, see Sidney Ahlstrom, *A Religious History of the American People*, 2nd edition (New Haven: Yale, 1972), 293–94.
23. Martin Brecht, *Martin Luther: His Road to Reformation 1483-1521*, translated by James L. Schaaf (Philadelphia: Fortress, 1985), 328. Historian Franz Posset has pointed to early examples of "Lutheran" being used in a positive sense as early as 1519, as well; Franz Posset, *Unser Luther: Martin Luther aus der Sicht katholischer Sympathisanten* (Münster: Aschendorff, 2015), 18.
24. LW 45:70.
25. Martin Marty, *Martin Luther* (New York: Viking Penguin, 2004), 42.
26. Brecht, *Martin Luther: His Road to Reformation 1483-1521*, 154.

Poland, the Slovak Republic, and Slovenia, where the churches are officially known as the "Evangelical Church of the Augsburg Confession."

Despite these other options, the name "Lutheran" is the one used the most widely in English. Although it was initially given as an insult and seems to emphasize one individual—Luther—rather than diverse communities of believers, there is a fascinating aspect to Luther's own name that adds depth to this label.

As signs of their educational status, scholars of the period would sometimes adopt Greek or Latin versions of their names. Melanchthon, for instance, is a Greek version of the German name *Schwarzerd*, which means "black earth;" Agricola is a Latin version of the German name *Bauer*, meaning farmer or peasant. Further, because spelling was not standardized in the German language of the early 1500s, people could be fluid in how they spelled their names. In this vein, the eldest son of enterprising miner Hans Luder added an *h* to his name when he entered the University of Erfurt in 1501 in order "to suit the more elegant, academic usage: the student named Luder was entered in the university register as 'Martinus Ludher.'"[27] (In the German of the time, the *t* and the *d* in Ludher were interchangeable.)

In the weeks after the publication of the *95 Theses* in 1517, Martin Ludher started signing his name, "Martinus Eleutherius." This follows the academic style of taking a Latin or Greek name, as mentioned above. Even more: similar in sound and spelling to Luther, Eleutherius comes from the Greek for "the liberated one" or "freed person" (as in 1 Cor 7:22), a meaning which Luther clearly claimed for himself at the time.[28] Although he eventually settled on "Luther" as the standard spelling of his family name, the freedom and liberation of Eleutherius could now be said to belong to his name.

What's in a name? More than simply interpreting "Lutheran" as followers of a single person, Lutherans today might claim the name as

27. Heiko Oberman, *Luther: Man between God and the Devil*, translated by Eileen Wallliser-Schwarzbart (New Haven, CT: Yale, 1989), 86.

28. Berndt Hamm, *The Early Luther: Stages in a Reformation Reorientation*, translated by Martin Lohrmann (Grand Rapids, MI: Eerdmans, 2014), 167–68 and footnote 36.

one that describes those who have been set free through the gospel. Already in these names—Evangelical and Lutheran—we see how the title and title page of the *Book of Concord* introduce us to a set of beliefs that are built upon the liberating gospel of Jesus Christ.

## Table of Contents

Moving from the cover and title page, we now open the *Book of Concord* and look at its contents. These are:

Preface to the *Book of Concord* (1580)
    The Three Ecumenical Creeds
    *The Augsburg Confession* (1530)
    *Apology of the Augsburg Confession* (1531)
    *The Smalcald Articles* (1537)
    *Treatise on the Power and Primacy of the Pope* (1537)
    *The Small Catechism* (1529)
    *The Large Catechism* (1529)
    *Formula of Concord* (1577)[29]

After a preface introducing the book's history and goals, the political and theological leaders who put together the *Book of Concord* wanted to reaffirm that Lutherans saw themselves as belonging to the wider Christian tradition and had never wanted to deviate from the faith of the apostles.

For this reason, the first theological documents in the *Book of Concord* are three creeds of the early church: the Apostles' Creed, which developed from the baptismal rites of the Latin Church; the Nicene Creed, composed at the ecumenical councils held in Nicaea (325) and Constantinople (381); and the Athanasian Creed, a work which contains a strong affirmation of the Trinity and had been held in high regard in the Latin Church since the time of Charlemagne (ca. 800). This last statement of faith was probably written in southern France around the year 500 and not (as had been traditionally assumed) by the fourth-

---

29. BC v.

century bishop Athanasius, though that attribution was still unchallenged in the time of the Reformation.[30] As novel as Lutherans may have appeared to the wider Christian world around them, the creeds were included in the *Book of Concord* in order to show that Lutherans understood themselves as members of what the Nicene Creed describes as "the one, holy, catholic, and apostolic church."

Continuing through the table of contents, the *Augsburg Confession* of 1530 follows the ancient creeds. It is the first of the Reformation-era texts to appear in the *Book of Concord* because it is the one most widely viewed as the central expression of Lutheran teaching. Already in the 1530s it had become the standard statement of Evangelical Lutheran faith, practice, and unity. Although it involved a high degree of collaboration, the *Augsburg Confession* was primarily composed by Philip Melanchthon. It is sometimes also called "the *Augustana*" from its Latin title *Confessio Augustana*.

As mentioned above, events taking place in the city of Augsburg required more than just theological definitions or defenses. In the tense political situation that Lutherans were facing, the *Augsburg Confession* was both a confession of faith and a plea to the Church of Rome to tolerate these evangelical reforms, which Lutherans believed were founded squarely on the person of Christ, the scriptures, and the witness of the church across the centuries. Because it originally aimed to stress catholicity and Christian unity, the *Augsburg Confession* still retains much of that open and ecumenical feel, even as it expresses the passion and conviction of the early years of the Reformation.

If the *Augsburg Confession* was meant to show Lutheran harmony with the wider Christian tradition, Melanchthon's *Apology to the Augsburg Confession* shows the tenacity with which he and his colleagues would defend their views. After the presentation of the *Augsburg Confession* on June 25, 1530, Emperor Charles asked the theologians around him who were loyal to Rome to write a response. The group included Johann Eck and Johannes Cochlaeus, theologians who by that time had been working against Luther and evangelical reforms for more than a

---

30. BC 21, editors' introduction.

decade. In the autumn of 1530, Charles officially accepted this Roman "Confutation of the Augsburg Confession," thereby rejecting the Lutheran position. He gave the Lutherans until the following spring to comply, after which there would likely be war.[31] Though a war between Charles and the Lutherans did not break out until 1546, it remained a very real possibility in the intervening years.

Melanchthon's *Apology* came as a vigorous reply to the Roman Confutation. It revolves around the conviction that the evangelical teaching of justification by faith alone rightly stands at the center of Christian life and the church's mission. In addition to supporting the Lutherans' theological views, the *Apology* also served the political purpose of trying to extend the debate: Lutherans had not yet agreed with the pronouncements of Roman church officials and wanted to keep their protest alive. The two most detailed topics in the *Apology* are Melanchthon's defense of justification by faith alone and the Lutheran view of repentance, which was the theological issue that had launched Luther's protest against indulgences in the first place.

The next work in the *Book of Concord* is the *Smalcald Articles*, named after the town where these articles were presented and discussed. Luther wrote them in late 1536 and early 1537 at the invitation of Elector John Frederick of Saxony, who had a twofold purpose for this document. First, John Frederick wanted a theological statement from Luther ready to share in case the papacy called an open council of the church; second, he wanted an updated confession of Luther's personal faith and teaching. As Luther was again deathly ill in late 1536 and early 1537, this work is sometimes called Luther's "last theological will and testament," even though he survived those illnesses to live for nearly another decade.[32]

For almost four hundred years (including already in 1580), people believed that the *Treatise on the Power and Primacy of the Pope* was written

---

31. Arand, Kolb and Nestingen, 124.
32. Reformation history William R. Russell popularized this description of the Smalcald Articles as Luther's "last testament" in works like: William R. Russell, *Luther's Theological Testament*, and William R. Russell, "The Smalcald Articles: Luther's Theological Testament," in *Lutheran Quarterly* 5 (Autumn 1991), 277–96.

by Luther as an addition to the *Smalcald Articles*. Actually, Melanchthon wrote this treatise for those same discussions in Smalcald in 1537. It was meant to serve as a supplement not to the *Smalcald Articles* but as an extension of the *Augsburg Confession*, which—in its desire to maintain unity with Rome—had not included an article on the Lutheran view of the papacy. It is another example of Melanchthon's great ability to identify and explain the main issues at stake, and to do so in a way consistent with Luther's thought. Because the *Smalcald Articles* and the *Treatise* have been identified with each other for so long, this book will continue the tradition of discussing them together.

Luther's *Small* and *Large Catechism*s come next. Published in 1529, they are the earliest works in the *Book of Concord* to have been written, though the *Augsburg Confession*'s status as the primary expression of Lutheran faith and practice means it comes first. Still, in many churches that did not adopt the entire *Book of Concord*—in Danish and Norwegian Lutheranism, for instance—the *Small Catechism* has long been included as a normative statement of faith together with the *Augustana*.

Luther wrote these catechisms to teach the basics of Christian faith to regular people. The *Small Catechism* in particular was meant for daily use in homes, schools and congregations. Luther discovered the need for such a down-to-earth resource after he visited congregations around Saxony in the late 1520s, taking stock of the worship life of area parishes. "Dear God, what misery I beheld!" he wrote. "The ordinary person, especially in the villages, knows absolutely nothing about the Christian faith, and unfortunately many pastors are completely unskilled and incompetent teachers."[33] A clear, simple, and "remember-able" presentation of Christianity was sorely needed.

Accessible to young and old, new and experienced Christians alike, the *Small Catechism* remains a spiritual treasure in many ways. First, it met its goal of presenting the faith in simple and memorable ways; generations of Lutherans have lived according to its clear, Bible-based instruction. Second, it included elements that we might today describe

---

33. SC 347.2.

as typical of multimedia resources. Its small size meant that it was portable. Early editions added pictures from the workshop of Wittenberg artist Lucas Cranach to illustrate Bible stories and scenes from church life that relate to the text. Early catechisms were available as posters, another visually accessible format. The *Small Catechism* can also be called a "social media" tool (in contrast to one-way "broadcast media"), because it was based on back-and-forth communication and learning: it could be used as a prayer book, an educational tool, a preaching aid, and a conversation starter. Luther himself used it in all of these ways.

Based on sermons that Luther preached in Wittenberg in 1528, the *Large Catechism* was published slightly before the *Small Catechism*.[34] Although still written with the average pastor and parishioner in mind, many ideas that are condensed in the *Small Catechism* receive more detailed treatment in the larger one. As the third work written by Luther in the *Book of Concord*, the *Large Catechism* reveals Luther's great ability to explain complex ideas in understandable ways.

Considering the complicated ideas that often surrounded the doctrinal debates of the period, it is worth noticing here that Lutherans have included practical resources in their collection of core writings. Books for regular Christians—including children—stand alongside sophisticated works of theology. This says something important about how Lutherans view the relationship between theology and daily faith: head, heart, and hand always need to learn, grow and serve together. Additionally, Christian faith is for all people in all stations and stages of life, not just for religious elites or theological specialists.

Finalized in 1577, the *Formula of Concord* was written because new controversies had arisen in the decades after Luther's death. Like Luther's *Large Catechism*, it began as a sermon series, though it received more revision on its way to publication. The *Formula* has two parts. The longer *Solid Declaration* is a prose examination of twelve doctrinal topics. It was composed by a group of pastors and theologians who represented different territories and theological backgrounds across

34. LW 51:133–93.

Germany. Because the *Solid Declaration* is relatively long and complicated, there is a second version, the *Epitome of the Formula of Concord*, which presents a summary of these discussions. It was written at the request of political leaders who did not want to read so much theology![35]

As mentioned above, the 1577 *Formula of Concord* and the 1580 publication of the *Book of Concord* united many, but not all, of the regional churches of the *Augsburg Confession*, giving the *Formula of Concord* a mixed legacy. It is viewed by some as the beginning of Lutheran Orthodoxy, a period often negatively identified with inward-looking projects to "develop a systematic theology designed to demonstrate the scientific truth of Lutheranism."[36] That is, the *Formula* can be read as a document that lifts up a particular Lutheran way of being Christian at the expense of others.

At the same time, rich Lutheran works of spirituality, science, and art appeared in those years, including the devotional writings of Johann Arndt, the hymns of Paul Gerhard, the compositions of J.S. Bach, and the astronomical research of Johannes Kepler. Despite these and other examples of popular spirituality and higher education, a negative characterization of the Lutheran Orthodox period remains. Interpretations of the *Formula of Concord* often play into this narrative by focusing on the dogmatic and controversial side of the *Formula* at the expense of its rich spiritual, pastoral and ecumenical insights.

The *Formula of Concord* is also sometimes guilty by association with what historians now call the "era of confessionalization." In this relatively recent historical field of study, scholars examine the ways in which the religious teaching of the period "helped to consolidate the power of the early modern state and to make Christianity a servant of the political process."[37] As this introduction has already pointed out, political events certainly and explicitly propelled the writing of documents like the *Augsburg Confession*, the *Smalcald Articles*, and the

---

35. BC 484, editors' introduction.
36. Eric Gritsch, *A History of Lutheranism* (Minneapolis: Fortress, 2002), 114.
37. Scott Hendrix, *Recultivating the Vineyard: The Reformation Agendas of Christianization* (Louisville: Westminster John Knox, 2004), 157.

*Formula of Concord.* For this reason, a good understanding of the political contexts surrounding the Lutheran Confessions is a helpful aid for interpreting the documents.

Even as the Lutheran reformers addressed important political realities, however, they also passionately shared their spiritual beliefs with integrity and care. Rather than undermining the spiritual side of these works, the obvious relationship between politics and religion in the Lutheran Confessions invites us to notice that passionate spiritual beliefs often take place in the messy complications of real life, including the social and political sides of our lives. While careful scrutiny of the relationship between religious and secular power remains critical, this study will keep a twofold focus on these writings both as expressions of spiritual faith and as genuine contributions to public discourse about what it means to serve the common good.

## Overview

To restate the thesis: the *Book of Concord* offers contemporary readers a rich and lively witness to Christian faith, spirituality, and service. To advance this main point, Chapter 2 will lift up themes of the early Reformation that provide a basis for understanding the *Book of Concord*. Chapter 3 then begins our chronological study of the documents in the *Book of Concord*, starting with Luther's catechisms. Chapter 4 studies the *Augsburg Confession*, while Chapter 5 covers Melanchthon's *Apology of the Augsburg Confession*. Chapter 6 returns to Martin Luther and his *Smalcald Articles*, along with Melanchthon's *Treatise on the Power and Primacy of the Pope*.

Chapter 7 then examines the *Formula of Concord* as a test case: how did a later generation of church leaders understand and express the evangelical faith they inherited? Is the *Formula of Concord* the end of Luther's lively Reformation and the beginning of a dry period of dogmatism and conformity? Or did it still communicate the pastoral and spiritual energy of the early Reformation? To such questions, Chapter 7 offers evidence that the *Formula of Concord* does indeed reflect, share and teach a passionate spirituality and concern for people's bodies and souls.

An epilogue provides a conclusion to this study of the *Book of Concord*, with observations on its continued relevance and usefulness for individuals and communities in the twenty-first century. Throughout this book, I hope that readers encounter lively examples of spirituality and service that positively inform faith and practice today.

2

———

# Themes in the Early Lutheran Reformation

## "Love and Zeal for the Truth"

October 31, 2017, marks five hundred years since Martin Luther changed the course of western civilization with his *95 Theses*, also entitled, "A Disputation on the Power and Efficacy of Indulgences." Why did Luther write against indulgences? In exchange for money or activities like going on a pilgrimage or participating in a crusade, indulgences promised sinners forgiveness from the penalty of their sins, including penalties that would need to be paid in the afterlife in purgatory. Indulgences were particularly open to misuse and corruption because they connected money and salvation.[1]

Luther did not intend for his theses (points for discussion) to mark the beginning of a new era. Nevertheless, their potentially dramatic force already appears in Thesis 1, which evokes the moment in Matthew 4 when Jesus returned from his time alone in the wilderness to begin his public ministry. Luther's opening thesis states: "When our

1. Brecht, *Martin Luther: His Road to Reformation 1483-1521*, 175–83.

Lord and Master Jesus Christ said, 'Repent,' he willed the entire life of believers to be one of repentance."[2]

Luther's protest against indulgences resonated with several spiritual and social concerns of the day. On the spiritual side, indulgences were connected with the church's teaching about penance (how sins are forgiven), justification (how people are made right with God), and salvation (eternal life with God).[3] Luther's critiques, therefore, challenged several key aspects of religious teaching and practice. Socially, people of the time had long questioned the unique rights and privileges that the clergy and the church hierarchy enjoyed; Luther's protest of indulgences tapped into general critiques of the institutional church and local German efforts toward more self-governance in political and church matters.[4] Further, by criticizing this specific sale of indulgences (the St. Peter's indulgence), Luther was challenging a financial system that profited people at the highest levels of society at the expense of poor and anxious souls. Those who profited most directly comprised a complicated web that included nobility, the papacy, and the banking industry.

Under the banner of evangelical freedom, Luther's protest captured the attention of diverse groups of people. Evidence of Luther's immense popularity at the time can be seen in the fact that, by the early 1520s, "over three-fourths of the books in print in Germany had been written by Luther."[5]

For all the excitement surrounding them, the dramatic moments of Luther's early career grew from his basic desire to remain accountable to the Bible, intellectual honesty, and the Christian tradition. This sense of responsibility to the Bible and to reasonable thinking appeared in Luther's introduction to the *95 Theses*. Setting the stage for the points he was about to make, Luther wrote:

Out of love and zeal for the truth and the desire to bring it to light,

---

2. LW 31:25, with a reference to Matt 4:17.
3. On the *95 Theses* as a Reformation document, see Hamm, chapter 4.
4. For more on the political situation at the time, see Carter Lindberg, *The European Reformations* (Malden, MA: Blackwell, 1996), 53; and Oberman, *Luther*, 14.
5. Arand, Kolb, and Nestingen, 73.

the following theses will be publicly discussed at Wittenberg under the chairmanship of the reverend father Martin Lutther [sic], Master of Arts and Sacred Theology and regularly appointed Lecturer on these subjects at that place. He requests that those who cannot be present to debate orally with us will do so by letter.[6]

Luther was eager to discuss his ideas with larger church communities, including his university and local bishops, to whom he mailed copies on the famous date of October 31, 1517. He appealed to his vocation as a doctor of theology to show that he was speaking from a position of public accountability. Through his study of the Bible, his engagement with the Christian tradition and his pastoral work in Wittenberg, Luther had found something important to share with the church of his time. Through the relatively new technology of the printing press, his insights quickly spread across Germany and the rest of Europe. His love and zeal for the truth caught the attention of an eager public.

Luther expressed a similar accountability to scripture and reason when he was on trial a few years later in front of Holy Roman Emperor Charles V. At that imperial diet in the city of Worms in April 1521, Luther again expressed his goal of remaining faithful to the Bible and "clear reason." Replying to the imperial demand that he renounce his writings, Luther said:

> Since then your serene majesty and your lordships seek a simple answer, I will give it in this manner, neither horned nor toothed: Unless I am convinced by the testimony of the Scriptures or by clear reason... I am bound by the Scriptures I have quoted and my conscience is captive to the Word of God. I cannot and I will not retract anything, since it is neither safe nor right to go against conscience. I cannot do otherwise, here I stand, may God help me, Amen.[7]

This emphasis on accountability to scripture, communal conversation, and clear reason remained a hallmark of Lutheran theology—including in the *Book of Concord*—long after these dramatic moments in Luther's early career had passed. While Luther possessed charismatic personal traits as a leader, preacher, and writer, the Reformation movement

6. LW 31:25.
7. LW 32:112. The phrase "here I stand" is lacking from some accounts.

that grew around him aimed first of all to remain faithful to the Bible, the careful use of reason, and pastoral concern for hearts, consciences, bodies, and souls. In such a setting, Luther's famous appeal to conscience was not a claim for subjective, individualist thinking; on the contrary, it represented a plea for open discussion of well-grounded intellectual and spiritual commitments that affect both individuals and communities.

Though Luther is rightly remembered for the dramatic stands of his early career, it is worth remembering what he was standing on and standing for. Luther was standing on a biblical faith in Christ that he had tried and tested for several years.[8] From this scriptural and intellectual foundation about a freedom that comes from faith alone in Christ alone, Luther's convictions could not be shaken by his opponents' appeals to longstanding traditions or earthly authority, as weighty and powerful as those forces were.

## The Early Luther and Later Lutheranism

Did the passion of the early Luther survive into the later Lutheran tradition? In many ways, the years that followed Luther's early career saw increasing discord rather than harmony among various reforming movements: Luther got entangled with the violence of the Peasants' Wars of 1524–25, he parted ways with "the prince of humanists" Erasmus of Rotterdam in 1525, and he could not agree with the view of the Lord's Supper held by other reformers like Zwingli. The end of the 1520s did not bring increased peace and mutual understanding.

Lutherans reached important agreements in 1536 with south German reformers in the *Wittenberg Concord*, and with representatives of the English Church through the *Wittenberg Articles*. Nevertheless, the next decades similarly brought the continued threat of war with Emperor Charles, deepened divisions with both Rome and other reforming movements, and new controversies among Lutherans themselves. By the time of Luther's death in early 1546, Lutheranism

---

8. On Luther's early career and his development as a reformer, see Hamm, chapters 1–3 and Brecht, *Martin Luther: His Road to Reformation 1483–1521*, chapters 2–6.

might well have surrendered the spark that launched Luther's impassioned and liberating Reformation only a few decades earlier.

Many studies of the Reformation tell precisely this story: Luther's inspirational "love and zeal for the truth" faded and devolved into the dull decrees of a bureaucratic church. Diarmaid MacCulloch, for instance, has claimed that the writings of the early Luther were not included in the *Book of Concord* because "they might prove too disruptive of the actual end result of Luther's Reformation," in which Lutheranism "took on the shape of the late medieval western Church in the north. It now represented a successful effort by much of the ruling caste in Europe to graft a religious revolution onto traditional forms of life, to ensure the stability of their rule."[9] In McCulloch's view, the vitality of Luther's early reforming efforts vanished. In its place, the oppressive structures that Luther had worked so hard to overturn were simply reintroduced in Lutheran dress by the ruling classes.

Similarly, in his book *The Cross in Our Context*, theologian Douglas John Hall asserted that Lutherans have long failed to live out the dynamic faith of Luther's theology. For instance, in wondering why a Reformation teaching as vibrant as Luther's "theology of the cross" (discussed later in this chapter) remained relatively unknown and underutilized, Hall explained that this is largely because Lutherans themselves have been reluctant "to give this tradition much more than a theoretical or reverential nod."[10] A footnote later in the same chapter blames Philip Melanchthon for this withering of Luther's lively faith.[11] In another of his books, Hall blamed Luther himself: "The most disappointing aspect of Luther's thought and life is his failure to apply his *theologia crucis* [theology of the cross] . . . to social structures in general and to the church in particular."[12] According to this line of

---

9. Diarmaid MacCulloch, *The Reformation* (New York: Viking, 2003), 343.
10. Douglas John Hall, *The Cross in Our Context: Jesus and the Suffering World* (Minneapolis: Fortress, 2003), 14.
11. Hall, *The Cross in Our Context*, 19 and note 15 (233).
12. Douglas John Hall, *Lighten Our Darkness: Towards an Indigenous Theology of the Cross*, revised edition (Lima, OH: Academic Renewal Press, 2001), 125. See also Hall, *The Cross in Our Context*, 173–74: "[Luther] understood very well that a theology of the cross that does not translate at once into an ecclesiology of the cross would be a contradiction in terms . . . If in the end his theology did fail to fashion such an alternative ecclesiology, if still today people in Lutheran and other Protestant

thinking, Lutherans have been failing to live out their faith in Jesus Christ since the start of their own Reformation!

Respectfully disagreeing with these assessments, this book proposes alternative interpretations of Lutheran history and teaching. For one thing, the works within the *Book of Concord* all include serious suggestions for how to reform "social structures in general" and "the church in particular." Additionally, interested readers might study Carter Lindberg's *Beyond Charity: Reformation Initiatives for the Poor*, which examines the history of how Lutherans did, in fact, successfully translate their new evangelical theology into effective social reforms and church structures.[13] Primary sources that explain both the theology and strategy for Lutheran social reform are also now available in a two-volume translation of Johannes Bugenhagen's works. Bugenhagen, who worked alongside Luther and Melanchthon for decades, wrote many of the church orders (similar to contemporary church constitutions) that described how faith and reform fit together and can be put into practice. These connections are especially visible in writings like Bugenhagen's 1526 letter to Hamburg and the Braunschweig Church Order of 1528.[14]

Among many other possible examples, the activity of Lutheran Services in America (LSA), an umbrella organization of North American Lutherans and their nonprofit social ministries, gives a sign of the vitality of Lutheran faith and practice in the present. In 2014, the collective annual income for LSA was $21 billion, with more than 6 million people served across the United States and the Caribbean.[15] These activities often had their starts in the efforts of local congregations and continue to serve as a natural outgrowth of

---

settings can talk about the theology of the cross while contenting themselves with a church of glory, it is only because the Protestantism that Luther and the others championed itself became so quickly the new establishments of northern Europe and, later, the European satellites [colonies]."

13. Carter Lindberg, *Beyond Charity: Reformation Initiatives for the Poor* (Minneapolis: Fortress, 1993). A similar study in German is Tim Lorentzen, *Johannes Bugenhagen als Reformator der öffentlichen Fürsorge* (Tübingen: Mohr Siebeck, 2008). Translated, the title would read, "Johannes Bugenhagen as Reformer of the Public Welfare."

14. Johannes Bugenhagen, *Selected Writings, Volumes 1 and 2*, edited and translated by Kurt K. Hendel (Minneapolis: Fortress, 2015), especially 1:191–359 and 2:1181–1399.

15. http://www.lutheranservices.org/AboutUs.

Lutheran faith and ministry. There are many more stories to be told about the practical effects of the Lutheran witness. This study will continue to lift up the relationship between faith and action as it arises in the *Book of Concord*. Instead of disappearing, readers might be surprised to see the extent to which the early energy of the Reformation survived theologically and institutionally in ways that later generations would continue to build upon. Far from being a weakness of the tradition, Lutheranism offers a long legacy of connecting faith and direct action.

## Lutherans and the Bible

To return to the early Reformation, Luther's emphasis on the Bible is often mentioned as a reason why his work appealed to so many people. That is true, but perhaps not in the way people might imagine today. For one thing, the Bible was not "lost" in the Middle Ages. On the contrary, people in late medieval Europe lived in a world full of biblical images and concepts. If the majority of the population had limited access to the printed word and the Latin Bible, then stained-glass windows, paintings, statues and songs helped fill people's senses with biblical stories and Christian interpretations of the world.

One key difference between medieval and Reformation ways of engaging the Bible, however, arose through the insights of Renaissance humanism. Humanist scholars like Erasmus of Rotterdam and Rudolf Agricola started reading the Bible like students of literature read books today, asking questions like: What do the words really mean? What is the plot? What are these writings trying to teach us and how are they making their points? As indicated by the humanist motto *ad fontes*, scholars were going "back to the sources" to read the Bible in Greek and Hebrew, hearing it speak in fresh new ways.

This new humanist learning directly influenced the Reformation. In October 1512, Martin Luther became a doctor of theology. His educational background included training in medieval theology at the universities in Erfurt and Wittenberg, the daily devotional life of his observant monastic community, and a growing familiarity with the new linguistic tools provided by scholars like Johannes Reuchlin and Erasmus. In addition to all this, Luther cultivated an intimate personal knowledge of the Bible. For instance, when Johann von Staupitz, the local head of the Observant Augustinian order, first met Luther, Staupitz gave him the assignment of memorizing the Bible, a task Luther took to heart: in the early years of the Reformation, Luther was reading through the entire Bible twice a year.[16]

Philip Melanchthon's arrival to teach at Wittenberg in 1518 further connected humanism with Lutheran reforms. Melanchthon learned Greek as a boy, and although he had completed his master's program at the University of Heidelberg, he was not allowed to receive his degree when he was first eligible for it, because at fourteen years old he was deemed too young![17] Other early leaders of the Lutheran Reformation like Bugenhagen, Georg Spalatin, Urbanus Rhegius, and Justus Jonas shared similar educational backgrounds that combined devotional practice, scholarly rigor, and the use of humanist interpretive tools.

Already early in the Reformation, therefore, these diverse influences meant that Lutheran biblical interpretation and theological writing combined scholarly study with down-to-earth pastoral care for how the gospel message speaks to real people and communities. These traits gave enduring shape to the Lutheran reformers' engagement with scripture as the life-giving word of God that has something vital to say to people each time they encounter it, whether through worship, images, song, study, or prayer.

## What a Thing Is—What a Thing Does

From these backgrounds, the Lutheran reformers developed a way of reading the Bible that revolved around definitions and effects. When considering a biblical subject, reformers would ask the question "what is it?" in order to understand the concept at hand as clearly as possible.

---

16. Oberman, 136 and 173.
17. Robert Stupperich, *Melanchthon*, translated by Robert Fischer (Philadelphia: Westminster, 1965), 27.

Then they would look at the effects of that concept, asking "what does it do?" to learn the effects or results that come from knowing this biblical concept. Melanchthon explicitly connected this relationship between "what a thing is" and "what a thing does" in his early theological textbook, the *Loci Communes* of 1521, when he wrote, "to know Christ means to know his benefits."[18] For the Lutherans, biblical interpretation included first knowing what the Bible is saying and then understanding and even experiencing what God is doing through it in real life.[19]

We see this later in the same 1521 *Loci Communes*, where Melanchthon defined faith on the basis of Paul's letter to the Romans (1:16-17), explaining that "faith is nothing else than trust in the divine mercy promised in Christ." In almost the same breath, he then connected this definition with the effects of faith, that is, what faith does. "This trust in the goodwill or mercy of God first calms our hearts and then inflames us to give thanks to God for his mercy so that we keep the law willingly and gladly."[20] In this case, Melanchthon connected the definition of faith with its effects in such a way that faith never sits still as an abstract concept or doctrine; instead, to know what faith is also means participating in the effects and actions that come with trust in God.

Luther's *Small Catechism* similarly shows this move from what a thing is to what a thing does. In the sections on the sacraments, for instance, Luther started by asking, "What is baptism?" After giving a short definition and a citation from scripture, Luther then asked, "What gifts or benefits does baptism give?"[21] In this model, baptism *is* "water enclosed in God's command and connected with God's word." Then, as a gift of God that *does* something, baptism "brings about forgiveness of sins, redeems from death and the devil, and gives eternal salvation

---

18. Philip Melanchthon, *Loci Communes Theologici* in *Melanchthon and Bucer*, Wilhelm Pauck, ed. (Philadelphia: Westminster, 1969), 21.
19. For more on the relationship between what a thing is (*quid sit*) and what a thing does (*quid effectus*) in Melanchthon's methodology, see Timothy Wengert, *Human Freedom, Christian Righteousness* (Oxford: Oxford, 1998), 52–56.
20. Melanchthon, 92.
21. SC 359.1-6.

to all who believe it, as the words and promise of God declare."[22] Once again we see how closely ideas and actions work together in the Lutheran Confessions: baptism not only *is* something but it also *does* things in the lives of real people.

The lively relationship between "what a thing is" and "what a thing does" occurs throughout the *Book of Concord*. Though written about a decade after his early *Loci Communes*, for instance, Melanchthon's explanation of justification by faith in the *Apology of the Augsburg Confession* follows the same pattern. There he wrote that justifying faith "*is* that which assents to the promise [of God]." He then added that as a work of the Holy Spirit faith not only *is* something but it *does* things, too: it "*receives* the forgiveness of sins, *makes* us acceptable to God, and *brings* peace and tranquility to the conscience."[23]

Though there is no explicit "doctrine of scripture" in the *Book of Concord*, this twofold emphasis on faith and its effects serves as a central Lutheran way to read the Bible. Within the Lutheran Confessions, the Bible is not simply a source for knowing things about God or the world; much more, it testifies to what God has done and continues to do. In short, the Lutheran Confessions present scripture as the living Word of a loving God who speaks to real hearts through the power of the Holy Spirit. In the words of the *Formula of Concord*, the Bible is "the pure, clear fountain of Israel" which nurtures a living relationship with the Lord of grace, truth and life.[24]

## Law and Gospel

Using the reformers' own categories of "what a thing is" and "what a thing does," a new question arises: If scripture *is* the word of God, then what does this word *do*? Through their scholarly and devotional engagement with the Bible, the Lutheran reformers observed that when it comes to the saving relationship between God and humans, scripture does one of two things: it either speaks God's judgment

22. SC 359.1-6.
23. Ap 139.113–16, italics added.
24. SD 527.3.

against sin or it announces the divine promise of forgiveness, reconciliation and new life, received through faith in Christ. This is the Lutheran distinction between law and gospel. As Melanchthon wrote in the *Apology*:

> All Scripture should be divided into these two main topics: the law and the promises. In some places it communicates the law. In other places it communicates the promise concerning Christ, either when it promises that Christ will come and on account of him offers the forgiveness of sins, justification, and eternal life, or when in the gospel itself, Christ, after he appeared, promises the forgiveness of sins, justification and eternal life.[25]

Through the scriptures, the Holy Spirit tells the truth about God, our hearts and our world. By speaking truth through the law, the scriptures name and condemn the hurtful reality of human sin; through the gospel, the Holy Spirit announces the true and holy gifts of grace, mercy and life given freely to unholy people.

The Lutheran reformers believed that the Holy Spirit makes sure that the words of the Bible do what they need to do, either to tell the truth about human sin and lead us to repentance or to announce the good news of God's free justification of the ungodly through Christ. This means that the same passage can even be experienced as law or gospel, depending on the situation and the hearer.[26] For instance, Mary's song in Luke 1:46-55 includes the words, "[The Lord] has brought down the powerful from their thrones, and lifted up the lowly; he has filled the hungry with good things, and sent the rich away empty." In his commentary on this passage, Luther noticed that this single passage does two things: God announces judgment against the proud and powerful ones of the earth and promises comfort and plenty to the lowly and the poor. In the same verse, the proud are led to repentance and faith; the lowly are embraced with the promise of the gospel.[27] How a person experiences this passage will depend on which word they need to hear.

---

25. Ap 121.5. For more on the distinction between law and gospel in the *Apology*, see Ap 194.48–196.55.
26. Jaroslav Pelikan, *Luther the Expositor*, Luther's Works: Companion Volume (St. Louis: Concordia, 1959), 66.
27. For more on Luther's interpretation of the *Magnificat*, see LW 21:297–358, especially 339–49.

This law-and-gospel way of reading the Bible creates a relationship with scripture in which we can expect that God's word will be doing something to us: telling the truth about sin and the truth about God's grace; killing the old sinful self and raising up a new creation. On this last point, the Luther reformers were fond of citing Hannah's song in 1 Sam 2:6: "The Lord kills and brings to life; he brings down to Sheol and raises up."

Because the Lutheran reformers believed that this movement from death to life is the most important thing that the Holy Spirit is doing through the scriptures, modern controversies about fundamentalism and inerrancy are not central Lutheran questions. Those debates reached public prominence in the 1800s with the rise of natural sciences (including Darwin's theory of evolution) and historical-critical methods of studying the Bible.[28] In the *Book of Concord*, though, the Bible is not holy because it sets inerrant scientific standards; it is holy because it leads us into salvation, life, and a blessed relationship with the Lord of life. As people who understood the value of applying reason to the natural world for the common good, the Lutheran reformers did not pit faith against science. They viewed the Bible as a source for learning the truth about divine love and human nature, not as a textbook on the natural sciences. This provides a helpful alternative to the idea that we need to either accept or reject scripture on the basis of modern ideas of inerrancy. At the same time—convinced of the innate inability of humans to save themselves—the reformers were deeply skeptical of rationalist attempts to promise either spiritual or physical deliverance. In short, faith and reason each have their gifts to share, in their own ways.

In the Lutheran tradition—to borrow from the Great Commandment (Deut 6:5 and Mark 12:30)—people of faith are free to serve the Lord with all of their minds. Reading scripture as law and gospel provides a way to live every day through the lens of the Bible's ongoing

---

28. On biblical interpretation in the nineteenth century, see John Sandys-Wunsch, *What Have They Done to the Bible? A History of Modern Biblical Interpretation* (Collegeville, MN: Liturgical Press, 2005), chapter 7; and Jaroslav Pelikan, *Whose Bible Is It? A Short History of the Scriptures* (New York: Penguin, 2005), chapter 10.

conversation about dying to sin and rising into new life through Christ. This is another way for Christians to experience Luther's first thesis: "When our Lord and Master Jesus Christ said, 'Repent,' he willed the entire life of believers to be one of repentance."[29] Daily we die to the old self by honestly applying the law to our sinfulness and the brokenness of the world around us; daily we are raised into new life through faith in the gospel of Christ. We can include the best of our intellects in that journey with God by asking: how are our minds and our energies being used to care for creation and our neighbors?

It is important to note that the Lutheran distinction between law and gospel is not a distinction between the Old Testament and the New Testament. For instance, Luther often identified Gen 3:15 as the "proto-gospel," in which the promise of a savior was given to sinners, as the Lord God said to the serpent: "I will put enmity between you and the woman, and between your offspring and hers; he will strike your head, and you will strike his heel." As mentioned above, the Lutheran reformers also cherished Hannah's song (1 Samuel 2) as an example of God's word doing its work both to kill the old creature (law) and raise a new creation (gospel): "The Lord kills and brings to life; he brings down to Sheol and raises up." Lutherans found ample evidence of God's grace in the Torah, prophets, and psalms of the Hebrew Scriptures.

If gospel can appear in the Old Testament, law can also speak in the New Testament. For instance, Luther put law and gospel to work in the same passage as he preached on the Christmas story of Luke 2. This passage provides one of the highest instances of God's gracious action to save sinners: "There in the stable, without man or maid [to serve him], is the Creator of the world!"[30] At the same time, however, Luther did not let the lofty mystery of Christ's birth get in the way of also naming the sinful and selfish realities that we live with. Addressing his fellow Christians in Wittenberg, he said:

> There are many of you in this congregation who think to yourselves: "If only I had been there! How quick I would have been to help the Baby! I

---

29. LW 31:25.
30. Martin Luther, *Martin Luther's Christmas Book*, ed. by Roland Bainton (Westminster, 1948), 33.

would have washed his linen. How happy I would have been to go with the shepherds to see the Lord lying in the manger!" Yes, you would! You say that because you know how great Christ is, but if you had been there at that time you would have done no better than the people of Bethlehem! Childish and silly thoughts are these! Why don't you do it now? You have Christ in your neighbor. You ought to serve him, for what you do to your neighbor in need you do to the Lord Christ himself.[31]

Because the relationship between law and gospel is a Spirit-led conversation, the same text can speak to people in different ways, depending on what the Holy Spirit wants to do to hearers through the word. In this case, Luther echoed the angel's good tidings of great joy that God's savior was born in Bethlehem; at the same time, he did not get so lost in the wonder of the incarnation that he overlooked the self-satisfaction of those who delighted in their own Christmas piety while ignoring Christ's body as manifested in the needs of their neighbors.

How does a preacher know which word—law or gospel—to deliver at any given time? How does a reader of the Bible know what God may be saying through any given passage? If we respond by seeking a single correct answer, then we might either get lost in uncertainty or stuck in endless debates about whose interpretation is best. The Lutheran reformers' response, however, was to trust that the word of God will do what it intends to lead people to saving faith in God; as Isa 55:11 says, "so shall my word be that goes out from my mouth; it shall not return to me empty, but it shall accomplish that which I purpose, and succeed in the thing for which I sent it." The Holy Spirit will work both law and gospel in people's hearts as each are needed. With prayerful discernment and careful attention to the biblical text, preachers, readers, and hearers are invited to listen deeply for the beneficial words that will both identify the truth of sin in their lives and announce the truth of the gospel that sets them free to love God and serve others selflessly.

For this reason, a Lutheran "doctrine of scripture" parallels the sacraments in how it can be discussed in terms of what scripture is and what it does: it *is* God's word, and it *acts* in human lives "to kill

31. *Martin Luther's Christmas Book*, 32.

and to make alive" (1 Sam 2:6). In the Lutheran tradition, scripture is a fountain—"the pure, clear fountain of Israel"—in which our daily dying, washing and rising in the waters of baptism occur. Law and gospel therefore works as a dialectic—an ongoing conversation—rather than a static set of answers.

## Theologians of the Cross

At the heart of God's work to save sinners stands the cross of Jesus Christ. It is law and gospel at once, both the place of God's great confrontation with sin, violence, and death, and the site of God's victory over these forces. Speaking of his crucifixion, Jesus said, "And I, when I am lifted up from the earth, will draw all people to myself" (John 12:32). The cross reveals who God is and what God does: the Lord of life creates life out of death. Christ even laid down the most holy and righteous "form of God" so that we might live (Phil 2:5-11). How do Lutherans read the Bible? They read it through the cross, where God's creating, redeeming and sustaining work are happening all at once. Already in 1515 Luther preached a sermon in which he said:

> Whoever wants to read the Bible must make sure he is not wrong, for the Scriptures can easily be stretched and guided, but no one should guide them according to his emotions; he should lead them to the well, that is to the cross of Christ, then he will certainly be right and cannot fail.[32]

Going to the well of scripture—*ad fontes*—brings people to the cross, where the Triune God has delivered new life and reconciliation to a fallen world.

Early in his career, Luther described "theologians of the cross" in the 1518 *Heidelberg Disputation*. At this gathering of his fellow Augustinians, the newly famous—or infamous—Luther was invited to present theses for discussion and debate. With the law and gospel dialectic and the connection between "what a thing is" and "what a thing does" in the background, he described how having the cross at the center of the Christian message means more than just assenting to historical

32. WA 1.52, 15-18. Cited in Oberman, 173.

or theological knowledge about the crucifixion of Jesus of Nazareth. Instead, being a theologian of the cross means applying Christ's death to ourselves, both as God's judgment against sin and the announcement of unconditional forgiveness and reconciliation through Christ. In the *Heidelberg Disputation* this move to "what the cross does" appears in the following theses:

18. It is certain that man must utterly despair of his own ability before he is prepared to receive the grace of Christ.
19. That person does not deserve to be called a theologian who looks upon the invisible things of God as though they were clearly perceptible in those things which have actually happened [Rom 1:20].
20. He deserves to be called a theologian, however, who comprehends the visible and manifest things of God seen through suffering and the cross.
21. A theologian of glory calls evil good and good evil. A theologian of the cross calls the thing what it actually is.[33]

A theologian of the cross sees the world in ways that reverse our normal perspectives. What seems right, good and glorious in our conventional wisdom often turns out to be empty and vain, while what appears lowly in the eyes of the world reveals the lasting power of God: the Lord brings down the mighty and lifts up the lowly (Luke 1:52). The cross gives new eyes to see the truth of both the world's vanity and God's enduring love.

This grand reversal appears again in Luther's *Explanations of the Ninety-Five Theses*, written around the same time as the *Heidelberg Disputation* in early 1518.

> A theologian of the cross (that is, one who speaks of the crucified and hidden God), teaches that punishments, crosses, and death are the most precious treasury of all and the most sacred relics which the Lord of this theology himself has consecrated and blessed, not alone by the touch of his most holy flesh but also by the embrace of his exceedingly holy and

---

33. LW 31:40.

divine will, and he has left these relics here to be kissed, sought after, and embraced.[34]

Instead of looking for reconciliation through relics, indulgences, or their own good works, Luther sent people to embrace the treasure of Christ's suffering and death, where true life is found. Instead of looking for God in glorious places or getting right with God through religious transactions, the theology of the cross can be described as seeing God at work for us in the least likely places; it is God at work in human lowliness, shame, suffering, and even death.[35]

As a centering point for faith, the cross then provides a basis for understanding the many other great reversals of the Bible: barren Abraham and Sarah become parents of a great nation; the enslaved people of Israel are liberated from the all-powerful Pharaoh; a little brother grows up to be the great King David; the savior of the nations is born in a manger and raised in the insignificant town of Nazareth. These all share in the great reversal described in Phil 2:5-11, in which the one who shared the image of God set divinity and glory aside in order to take the form a servant and accept death, "even death on a cross."

Without itself being an ethical principle, the theology of the cross carries the same ethical implications as the "law and gospel" conversation above. Because the gospel is pure promise, salvation comes simply by trusting in Christ and not by any moral, spiritual, or ethical actions of ours. Does this mean that Lutheranism has no ethical edge? This critique arose very early in the Lutheran Reformation. In response, Luther and Melanchthon made a critical distinction between cause and effect. Though good works and ethical behavior do not cause salvation, they are blessed effects of salvation. Following Matt 7:18 and Matt 12:33, Luther emphasized that a "good tree bears good fruit." In fact, he believed that *only after* God's free justification of sinners can people truly begin to do the free good works of love for others that

---

34. LW 31:225.
35. Gordon Lathrop and Timothy Wengert, *Christian Assembly: Marks of the Church in a Pluralistic Age* (Minneapolis: Fortress, 2004), 25.

have no strings attached. He expressed this simultaneous freedom and service by saying, "A Christian is a perfectly free lord of all, subject to no one. A Christian is a perfectly dutiful servant of all, subject to all."[36] Both freedom and service are true effects of faith. To use an image from biology and the study of DNA: freedom and service are like the double helix of a Christian life; they are always distinct, yet neither is complete without the other.

As we will see, the *Book of Concord* teaches service to others as a blessed effect (not cause) of justification in many places: in articles on faith and good works in the *Augsburg Confession* and the *Smalcald Articles*, in Melanchthon's explanation of justification in the *Apology*, and in articles on righteousness, good works, and the uses of the law in the *Formula of Concord*. This book's next chapter on Luther's catechisms will also include discussion of good works as the fruit of faith.

Nevertheless, because there is no separate article or doctrine called "theology of the cross" or "Lutheran ethics" in the *Book of Concord*, some theologians have assumed that later Lutherans—and maybe even Luther himself—had forgotten these things and neglected the connection between the cross, justification by faith, and Christian lives of service. However, readers who look for the theology of the cross in the *Book of Concord* will most certainly find it. The Lutheran Confessions repeatedly announce the cross' twofold work of confronting sin and delivering the good news of a God who gives everything in order to win us back. The *Book of Concord* keeps the theology of the cross at the heart of the Lutheran Christian witness and continuously speaks of Christian life as the daily experience of liberation from sin and service to others.

## Learning from History: The School of the Cross

Before continuing with this study of the *Book of Concord*, it is important to name and address some aspects within it that readers today will quite rightly find objectionable. Rather than pretend that these hard

---

36. LW 31:344.

topics do not exist or can be explained away, the Lutheran tradition of "love and zeal for the truth" invites critical discussion and learning.

Most terribly, because Luther participated in the long history of Christian persecution of Jews by writing works against Judaism and the Jewish people, Lutherans extended anti-Jewish policies and ideologies, including the genocidal actions of Nazi Germany. The most infamous of Luther's works in this direction is a writing from 1543 entitled *On the Jews and Their Lies*, in which the reformer suggested that political authorities should burn synagogues, destroy books of Torah, close Jewish-owned businesses, and expel Jewish people.[37] There is no minimizing or mitigating these words from such an important historical figure as Luther.

Another instance of Lutheran complicity with injustice arose in the events surrounding the Peasants' Wars of 1524–25. In that time, Luther found himself (and put himself) in a very complicated situation: just as he was calling for the nobility to suppress popular uprisings by force, armed troops killed rebellious peasants by the thousands.[38]

Further negative legacies of the tradition include the common Reformation description of Islam as a punishment of the devil, the identification of the papacy as Antichrist, the blanket condemnation and persecution of Anabaptists and other "radical" branches of the Reformation, the continued assumption of a patriarchal worldview in Reformation writings, and later Lutheran participation in the slave trade and colonialism. Because these topics are so important, they each deserve and have received independent in-depth study; readers can learn more about them through the resources listed in these

---

37. LW 47:137-306, especially 267–92.
38. On Luther and the Peasants' War, see Martin Brecht, *Martin Luther: Shaping and Defining the Reformation, 1521-1532*, translated by James Schaaf (Minneapolis: Fortress, 1990), 172–94; and Lindberg, *The European Reformations*, 163–68.

footnotes.[39] Nevertheless, some words about these important matters belong here.

Regarding Lutheran participation in violence committed against Jews and Anabaptists, many Lutheran church bodies have issued official statements of repentance and apology.[40] Though these

---

39. For a study of Luther's work against a variety of theological adversaries, see Mark U. Edwards, Jr., *Luther and the False Brethren* (Stanford: Stanford, 1975) and Mark U. Edwards, Jr., *Luther's Last Battles: Politics and Polemics, 1531-46* (Philadelphia: Fortress, 1983).

Luther's harshest writings against the Jews appear in *On the Jews and Their Lies* (1543), LW 47:137–306, especially pages 265–72. More detailed studies of Luther's (and Lutheran) anti-Semitism can be found in Brooks Schramm and Kirsi Stjerna, *Martin Luther, The Bible, and the Jewish People: A Reader* (Minneapolis: Fortress, 2012); Brecht, *Martin Luther: The Preservation of the Church 1532-1546*, 333–51; Heiko Oberman, *The Roots of Anti-Semitism in the Age of Renaissance and Reformation*, translated by James I. Porter (Philadelphia: Fortress, 1984); and Steven Ozment, *A Mighty Fortress: A New History of the German People* (New York: HarperCollins, 2004), 94–100.

Key writings by Luther around the time of the Peasants' War include *A Sincere Admonition by Martin Luther to All Christians to Guard against Insurrection and Rebellion* (1522), LW 45:57–74; *Temporal Authority: To What Extent It Should Be Obeyed* (1523), LW 45:81–129; *Admonition to Peace: A Reply to the Twelve Articles of the Peasants in Swabia* (1525), LW 46:17–43; *Against the Robbing and Murdering Hordes of Peasants* (1525), LW 46:49–55; and *An Open Letter on the Harsh Book against the Peasants* (1525), LW 46:63–85. See also Edwards, *Luther and the False Brethren*, chapter 3; and Brecht, *Martin Luther: Shaping and Defining the Reformation: 1521-1532*, 172–94.

Studies of Lutheran views of Islam include: Brecht, *Martin Luther: The Preservation of the Church 1532-1546*, 351–57; Adam Francisco, *Martin Luther and Islam: A Study in Sixteenth-century Polemics and Apologetics* (Leiden: Brill, 2007); David Grafton, *Piety, Politics, and Power: Lutherans Encountering Islam in the Middle East* (Eugene, OR: Pickwick, 2009), especially chapter 2; and Paul Rajashekar, *Luther and Islam: An Asian Perspective* (Göttingen: Vandenhoeck & Ruprecht, 1990).

On the negative relationship that developed between Luther and Rome, see Scott Hendrix, *Luther and the Papacy: Stages in a Reformation Conflict* (Philadelphia: Fortress, 1981). On the relationship between Lutherans and more radical reformers, see Edwards, *Luther and the False Brethren*, chapter 4; Eric W. Gritsch, *Reformer without a Church: Thomas Muentzer* (Philadelphia: Fortress, 1967); Ronald Sider, ed., *Karlstadt's Battle with Luther: Documents in a Liberal-Radical Debate* (Philadelphia: Fortress, 1978); and George H. Williams, *The Radical Reformation* (Philadelphia: Westminster, 1962).

Among many recent studies on the roles and activities of women during the Reformation, see Susan Karant-Nunn and Merry Wiesner-Hanks, *Luther on Women: A Sourcebook* (Cambridge: Cambridge, 2003); Katharina Schütz Zell, *Church Mother: The Writings of a Protestant Reformation in Sixteenth-Century Germany*, edited by Elsie McKee (Chicago: Chicago, 2006); Kirsi Stjerna, *Women and the Reformation* (Malden, MA: Blackwell, 2008); and Merry Wiesner-Hanks, *Women and Gender in Early Modern Europe* (Cambridge: Cambridge, 2008).

On Lutherans and colonialism, see Walter Altmann, *Luther and Liberation: A Latin American Perspective*, translated by Mary Solberg (Minneapolis: Augsburg Fortress, 1992); L. DeAne Lagerquist, *The Lutherans* (Westport, CT: Praeger, 1999), chapter 2; Fidon R. Mwombeki, "The Theology of the Cross: Does It Make Sense to Africans?" and Ambrose Moyo, "Reconciliation and Forgiveness in an Unjust Society," in *The Gift of Grace: The Future of Lutheran Theology*, edited by Niels Henrik Gregersen, Bo Holm, Ted Peters, and Peter Widmann (Minneapolis: Fortress, 2005); and Winston D. Persaud, "Lutheran Theology and Postcolonial Caribbean: Theological Themes in Context," in *The Future of Lutheranism in a Global Context*.

40. For instance, "Declaration of ELCA to Jewish Community" (1994), http://download.elca.org/ELCA ResourceRepository/Declaration_Of_The_ELCA_To_The_Jewish_Community.pdf?_ga=1.84621785 .1311974491.1433446633; and "Declaration of the Evangelical Lutheran Church in America on the Condemnation of Anabaptists," http://download.elca.org/ELCA Resource Repository/

statements can never remove the terrible wrongs committed, they begin to redefine our lives together in ways that might lead to greater truth and reconciliation. Intentional and respectful efforts at interfaith and ecumenical dialogue also continue to take place locally, nationally, and internationally. One prominent example of that work is the *Joint Declaration on the Doctrine of Justification* (signed in 1999), in which the Lutheran World Federation and the Vatican agreed to set aside the mutual condemnations from the sixteenth century that arose because of differing views of justification.[41]

For this study of the *Book of Concord*, it is crucial to state that learning from a tradition does not mean defending or maintaining its prejudices and errors. On the contrary, if Lutheranism teaches a daily dying to sin and rising in Christ, then Lutherans can honestly acknowledge sin, repent of it, and walk again in love of God and service to others. "Love and zeal for the truth" demands such honesty and repentance. Luther was no one's savior, nor are the confessional writings of the tradition he inspired. Instead—as these past Christians often said themselves—their enduring witness rests not in their greatness but in their pointing others to the eternal goodness of God in Christ, who came to call the lost, lift up the lowly and bring life out of death.

The Lutheran reformers called this kind of learning "the school of the cross."[42] The cross shows us sin in and around us. This recognition of sin can be painful, because it shows us the often ugly and terrible truth about ourselves and the unjust systems we participate in. Yet even as it absolutely condemns sin and injustice, the cross also sets sinners upon the path of truth, repentance, and service in word and deed. At its best, the Lutheran tradition does not shy away from this school of the cross but can boldly claim it. After all, Thesis 1 of what became the Lutheran movement states, "When our Lord and Master Jesus Christ said, 'Repent,' he willed the entire life of believers to be

Declaration_Of_The_ELCA_On_The_Condemnation_Of_Anabaptists.pdf. These actions have parallels on the international level through the Lutheran World Federation.

41. http://www.vatican.va/roman_curia/pontifical_councils/chrstuni/documents/rc_pc_chrstuni_doc_31101999_cath-luth-joint-declaration_en.html.

42. The phrase appears as such in Luther's *Lectures on Isaiah*, LW 17:325, and in many other forms throughout Luther and Melanchthon's writings.

one of repentance." As it did in 1517, love and zeal for the truth will continue to push us into hard topics and reveal new horizons of freedom and service.

3

------

# Luther's Catechisms:
# A Lifetime of Learning

If you want to teach the basics of Christian faith, where do you begin? When confronted with the need to give Christian instruction in down-to-earth ways, Martin Luther presented people with a catechism.

Although "catechism" is not itself a simple word, it describes what it is and what it does. The word catechism has "echo" inside of it. In the early church, new Christians would echo back what they were learning from experienced believers. For centuries before Luther in the medieval church, the content of this instruction revolved around the Apostles' Creed, the Lord's Prayer, and the Ten Commandments; sometimes other prayers like the *Ave Maria* were added.

The goal was for all people to claim the central ideas of the faith as their own: learn it, live it out, and let it echo in and around them. Catechisms teach the faith in such a way that it will resound and re-sound in people's hearts for a lifetime. While learning by hearing and repeating can sometimes seem like a shallow kind of rote memorization, it is also an ancient and effective way to learn something deeply. If you doubt this, just think of how many people today can remember their favorite songs or lines from movies through listening and repetition.

This chapter will show how Luther viewed his *Small Catechism* as a lifelong resource for faith, preaching, prayer, and stewardship. Similarly, his *Large Catechism* explains Christian faith in a way that is still engaging, understandable, and useful for pastors and adult learners today. Though they are not explicitly named, Lutheran themes of law and gospel, theology of the cross, and Christian service fill the catechisms. Additionally, although one might not consider a catechism as biblical commentary, each part of the catechism comes from the Bible: the commandments appear in Exodus 20 and Deuteronomy 5; the Lord's Prayer is in Matthew 6 and Luke 11; the institution of baptism and the Lord's Supper are described in the gospels and St. Paul's letters; and the Apostles' Creed was viewed by the Lutheran reformers as a summary of the Bible's teachings about who God is and what God does. In short, Luther's catechisms present a thoroughly Bible-based Christianity accessible to a wide variety of audiences. All these years later, Luther's catechisms remain vibrant spiritual and practical resources, based on the Bible and emphasizing the connections between faith and daily life.

## The Ten Commandments

The Ten Commandments reveal God's will for human life and establish the Lord's covenant with the people of Israel.[1] Beyond the passages in Exodus and Deuteronomy in which they appear, the commandments also provide the basis of much reflection and commentary in the Psalms and the prophets, as well as the writings of the New Testament. As Luther wrote about the first commandment, "the whole Scriptures have proclaimed and presented this commandment everywhere, emphasizing these two things, fear of God and trust in God."[2]

Luther also noticed that the commandments begin with what is most

1. Luther followed the medieval Catholic tradition in counting the prohibition against images as a subsection of the first commandment and counting two commands against coveting. Jewish, Eastern Orthodox, and Reformed traditions number the commandments differently.
2. LC 430.325.

important and proceed from there, starting with God's relationship with us. Thus the first three commandments teach people to honor the Lord with our hearts, words, and bodies: love the Lord above all else, speak truly to God and about God, and physically assemble to worship the Lord who made heaven and earth. The next commandments then address the most central aspects of human life: honoring parents and elders, caring for the physical lives of others (do not murder), supporting intimate relationships (do not commit adultery), respecting other people's belongings (do not steal), and upholding the reputation and good name of those around us (do not bear false witness).

Finally, the commandments end with words against coveting. To covet means to want other people's relationships or belongings for oneself. Luther interpreted these last commandments as aiming especially at the hearts of people who most want to be seen as righteous. Why? Because it is precisely such people who are most likely to invent schemes that have "the appearance of legality" in order to "cunningly filch something out of another's hand so that the victim is helpless to prevent it."[3] Therefore, these words against coveting are not simple repetitions of "do not steal" or "do not commit adultery," but rather warn even the most pious hearts and upstanding citizens to beware of their own selfish motives. In short, the Ten Commandments get to the core of who we are and where we put our trust.

## What Does It Mean to Have a God?

In the *Large Catechism*, Luther started his discussion of the first commandment by asking what it means to have a god. In a time like ours, when the existence of God is routinely questioned, Luther's discussion goes right to the heart of the matter. Not interested in theoretical proofs for or against the existence of God, Luther began very concretely: "A 'god' is the term for that to which we are to look for all good and in which we are to find refuge in all need. Therefore, to have a god is nothing else than to trust and believe in that one with

3. LC 426.300–306.

your whole heart."[4] In times of trouble and need, where do we turn for life, goodness, and help? Where do we find our deepest identity and meaning? In what or in whom do we trust? Whatever it is, that will be our god. In the face of so many other competing interests, the first commandment announces a relationship with the one Lord who created the heavens and the earth and has given us life.

As mentioned above, Luther believed that the commandments begin with the most important and go from there. "Thus the First Commandment is to illuminate and impart its splendor to all the others."[5] When trust in God comes first, then right prayer and worship follow. When trust in God rules our hearts, minds and bodies, then we are free to care for the lives and welfare of our neighbors with no strings attached. When trust in God is lacking, however, then whatever else we do comes from the wrong motives as we seek life from something other than our creator. For this reason, Luther wrote in his 1520 tract *The Freedom of a Christian*:

> You see that the first commandment, "You shall worship one God," is fulfilled by faith alone. Even if you were nothing but good works from the soles of your feet to the top of your head, you would not be righteous, worship God, or fulfill the first commandment . . . Therefore faith alone is the righteousness of a Christian and the fulfilling of the commandments. For the one who fulfills the first commandment easily fulfills the rest of them.[6]

Faith alone lets God be God and looks to the Lord for all good and for all life. Comparing that statement from *The Freedom of a Christian* with the *Large Catechism* written almost a decade later, we find Luther just as convinced that nothing but faith fulfills the first commandment.

> This is exactly the meaning and the right interpretation of the first and chief commandment, from which all the others proceed. This word, "You shall have no other gods," means simply, "You shall fear, love, and trust me as your one true God." For where your heart has such an attitude toward God, you have fulfilled this commandment and all the others.[7]

4. LC 386.2.
5. LC 430.325–26.
6. Luther, *The Freedom of a Christian*, 64.
7. LC 429–30.324.

Here is our first example of the radical "faith alone" emphasis of the early Luther very much alive and well in the *Book of Concord*. Considering that the *Large Catechism* began as sermons in Wittenberg, we also get an example of Luther's ability to explain what it means to have a God to the townspeople gathered in his congregation.[8] The difference between true faith in God and false belief is not an abstract distinction for theologians to work out. It is an intimate personal question for all people to consider daily: to whom do we turn for life, goodness, and help?

Following the commandments themselves, Luther's teaching puts trust in God first. If faith is not present, then we have put things out of order, despite our outward obedience to the other commands. That does not mean people cannot do nice or helpful things for their neighbors but it means that our motives will be faulty, beginning with the desire to play god and fix the world based on our own ideas and worldviews. This commandment excels at showing the presence of false gods in our lives, especially the ones that live in our own hearts. At the same time, the first commandment teaches that faith in God means knowing and giving thanks that life and love have already come freely to us from the Lord, out of pure grace alone.

## Honor Your Father and Your Mother

The strong emphasis on the first commandment helps us understand Lutheran views of freedom, authority, and service. Luther taught obedience to earthly rulers as a value connected to the fourth commandment, "Honor your father and your mother."[9] Although he did not cite it in the catechisms, he often supported this elsewhere with New Testament verses like Rom 13:1, "Let every person be subject to the governing authorities; for there is no authority except from God, and those authorities that exist have been instituted by God."[10] Luther's emphasis on respecting parents and other authority figures

8. See Luther's 1528 sermon on the first commandment; LW 51:138–41.
9. SC 352.8 and LC 405.141.
10. For instance, in the "Household Chart" (*die Haustafel* or table of duties) that Luther added to the *Small Catechism*; SC 365, with footnote 115.

has led to the critique that the Lutheran Reformation taught an almost blind obedience to secular authority, giving Lutherans no basis for resisting unjust rulers or laws.

Ironically, however, Luther is remembered as one of the greatest rebels in human history because of the stands he took against pope and emperor. How can this contradiction be? Some might say it was because Luther held others to standards he himself did not follow, or that he later abandoned the freedom he embraced earlier in the Reformation. Unfortunately, as works aimed at teaching the basics of the faith, the catechisms do not say much about complicated issues like when and how to resist unjust authority. Nevertheless, Luther approached this issue in the *Large Catechism* by speaking of the positive benefits that come from observing the fourth commandment and by describing obedience to human authority in light of the God-relationship that is the foundation of faith.

Given its prominence in the Ten Commandments as the first one that addresses human relationships, Luther believed that honoring parents was the best good deed a person can do. Even more amazing, humble children rather than spiritual elites fulfill this holiest of works most completely.[11] Following Eph 6:2-3 and the words that accompany the commandment itself, Luther pointed out, "This is the first commandment with a promise: 'so that it may be well with you and you may live long on the earth.'"[12] Further, extending this commandment to the wider social realm means that those who serve in their secular jobs also share in the holy work of this commandment. As Luther wrote:

> If this could be impressed on the poor people, a servant girl would dance for joy and praise and thank God; and with her careful work, for which she receives sustenance and wages, she would obtain a treasure such as those who are regarded as the greatest saints do not have. Is it not a tremendous honor to know this and to say, 'If you do your daily household chores, that is better than the holiness and austere life of all the monks'? How could

11. LC 401.107 and 112.
12. LC 404.133.

46

you be more blessed or lead a holier life, as far as works are concerned? ... You are a true nobleman if you are simply upright and obedient.[13]

While it may be possible to interpret this as a way of blessing the economic or social status quo, Luther here redefined work and service as sainthood and nobility. In modern terms, we might say that Luther affirmed the dignity of work and laborers of all kinds, a conviction which has profound implications for social policies about work, living conditions, and human rights.

To push this point, Luther ended this section by speaking directly to parents and authority figures. God does not give these positions of authority in order for them to be abused but so that servant leaders will care for those around them. Luther wrote that God "does not want scoundrels or tyrants in this office or authority; nor does he assign them this honor (that is, power and right to govern) so that they may receive homage."[14] This commandment, therefore, condemns bad leaders and holds them accountable for their poor leadership. Luther continued:

> But once again, the real trouble is that no one perceives or pays attention to this. Everyone acts as if God gave us children for our pleasure and amusement, gave us servants merely to put them to work like cows or donkeys, and gave us subjects to treat as we please, as if it were no concern of ours what they learn or how they live. No one is willing to see that this is the command of the divine Majesty, who will solemnly call us to account and punish us for its neglect. Nor is it recognized how very necessary it is to devote serious attention to the young. For if we want capable and qualified people for both the civil and the spiritual realms, we really must spare no effort, time, and expense in teaching and educating our children to serve God and the world.[15]

Instead of simply telling children and subjects that they owe respect to those in power over them, Luther ended his explanation with a forceful case that this commandment is equally about how those in authority tend to those who are in their care, whether that authority exists in

13. LC 406.145–47 and 407.148.
14. LC 409.168.
15. LC 409.130–410.172.

home, work, school, church, or government. Strongly denouncing the abuse of authority, Luther called for humane treatment of all people regardless of their age or social status and for education that serves the good of individuals and their communities.

These important themes of faithfulness and obedience will return in our discussion of the *Augsburg Confession*. For now, it is enough to notice that the catechisms provide biblically-based ways for understanding matters of power and respect, including reasons to critique unjust authority. We have also seen how the first commandment's emphasis on trust in God provides a foundation for how people treat one another.

## Commandments in Word and Image

Luther's decision to teach the faith through the few documents contained in the catechism (commandments, creed, Lord's Prayer, and sacraments) was not a way to limit people's exposure to the wider stories of scripture but to open it up. For instance, consider how many biblical stories involve some aspect of the Ten Commandments: people trusting or not trusting in God, people treating each other lovingly or badly. Lending visual support to the commandments' important role within the entire Bible, early editions of the *Catechism* (both *Large* and *Small*) were illustrated with related biblical stories, as listed below.[16]

First Commandment: Moses on the mountaintop, while the people worship the Golden Calf down below (Exodus 32).

Second Commandment: The blasphemy of Shelomith's Son (Leviticus 24).

Third Commandment: Violating the Sabbath (Numbers 15)

---

16. Images for the Ten Commandments appear in WA 30.1: 133, 139, 143, 147, 157, 161, 164, 169, and 175, respectively. Images for the creed appear in WA 30.1: 184 and 187. Images for the Lord's Prayer appear in WA 30.1: 198, 200, 202, 204, 206, 208, and 210. Also, images reproduced from the 1584 Latin version of the Book of Concord (slightly different from those in WA 30.1) appear throughout Timothy Wengert, *Martin Luther's Catechisms: Forming the Faith* (Minneapolis: Fortress, 2009). An image of the only extant page from the broadside (poster) edition of the *Small Catechism* appears in WA 30.1:241.

Fourth Commandment: Ham uncovers his father Noah's nakedness (Genesis 9).

Fifth Commandment: Cain kills his brother Abel (Genesis 4).

Sixth Commandment: David and Bathsheba (2 Samuel 11).

Seventh Commandment: The theft of Achan (Joshua 7).

Eighth Commandment: Suzanna unjustly accused (Suzanna)

Ninth Commandment: Jacob and Laban (Genesis 30)

Tenth Commandment: Joseph resisting Potiphar's wife (Genesis 39)

Through these images, the catechism engaged many parts of the Bible beyond the commandments themselves. In addition to these visual aids, Luther often referred to other parts of the Bible when he preached on the commandments. Moving between the Old and New Testaments, he related many of the commandments to Christ's words in the Sermon on the Mount (Matthew 5).[17] When preaching on coveting, Luther recalled the story of wicked King Ahab plotting to take Nabaoth's vineyard (1 Kings 21).[18] Far from viewing these commandments as static rules for life and holiness, Luther put them in conversation with the experiences of people throughout the Bible and into the present.

### Commandments and Faith

In this way, Luther's *Small Catechism* does not merely give rules to memorize or principles to follow blindly. Instead, it provides a basis for tending to a lifelong relationship with God. The commandments do this by guiding our daily reflection on how we are living with God, our neighbors, and ourselves. Do we look to God or something else for life? Do we honor the Lord with our words and actions? Do we respect the dignity and rights of the people around us? Are we following the rules on the outside but secretly wishing and scheming for more on the inside? These are the daily meditations that the commandments offer. In light of a long history of Christian interpretation of Judaism as

17. LW 51:152.
18. LW 51:161.

a religion of external rules, this dynamic, dialectical understanding of the commandments can also give Christians a more sympathetic view of the deeply relational side of Jewish faith and practice.

Viewing the commandments as part of an ongoing relationship with God further reminds us that God loves us before we fulfill any commandments and after we have failed to keep them. Indeed, Luther took Paul's summary of Eccl 7:20 and Ps 14:2-3 to state the truth about the human ability to live according to God's will: "There is no one who is righteous, not even one; there is no one who has understanding, there is no one who seeks God" (Rom 3:10). Faith is not about us proving how much we love God and others; it is about trusting the one who loved us first.

If faith is a relationship with God based in truth, then we can acknowledge both the blessing and the challenge of the commandments. On the goodness of the commandments, Luther wrote, "Here, then, we have the Ten Commandments, a summary of divine teaching on what we are to do to make our whole life pleasing to God. They are the true fountain from which all good works must spring, the true channel through which all good works must be done. Apart from these Ten Commandments, no action or life can be good or pleasing to God, no matter how great or precious it may be in the eyes of the world."[19] Shortly thereafter, though, Luther commented on those who think the commandments are easy to fulfill and that more spiritual fanciness than just these Ten Commandments is needed to be truly holy. Of such spiritual elitists, he wrote, "They fail to see, these miserable, blind fools, that no one is able to keep even one of the Ten Commandments as it ought to be kept."[20]

Which is it? Are the commandments a gift or a curse? Are they good rules for us to live by or are they so impossible to fulfill that they merely leave us condemned and empty? Lutherans can appear to be of two minds on this question. As mentioned in the opening chapter, however, the word "dialectic" provides a great help, because

19. LC 428.311.
20. LC 428.316.

the commandments indeed invite us into a holy lifelong conversation about the truth of sin and the truth of God's grace.

First, Luther admired the commandments as a great blessing and "the true fountain from which all good works must be done" (as cited above). But, because they show us that we are "miserable, blind fools" who cannot keep them, they are also brutal in their direct condemnation of our sin, weakness, self-righteousness and pride. Finally, having realized the sad truth about ourselves, the commandments send us back to the beginning: trust in God alone for life and love. While each of these moves is true on its own, they work together to invite daily reflection on God's will, human sin, and need, and our trust that God alone gives life.

To this end, Luther did not leave people either assuming that believers will easily fulfill the commandments or despairing about ever being right with God because of sin. Instead, after pointing out human weakness and inability to do what the commands require, he sent people to further consideration of the first commandment and the contemplation of what kind of God we have. When it comes to learning more about who our God is, Luther wrote, "Both the Creed and the Lord's Prayer must come to our aid, as we shall see later. Through them we must seek and pray for help and receive it continually."[21] Throughout the Bible, getting right with God (being justified) is not about people being perfect. Being made right is about a holy and loving God declaring that fallible people are forgiven, loved, and blessed simply because God says so. God's love of the ungodly is what changes the world, not human efforts to try and be like God.

For all these reasons, the commandments stand as a blessed guide for our relationships with God and others. Since the commandments do not directly assert this relational aspect in themselves, however, Luther pointed people to the promises of God as expressed in the Apostles' Creed and the Lord's Prayer.

---

21. LC 428.316.

## The Children's Creed

Scholars often remark that Luther was not a systematic theologian.[22] Though it is true that he did not write theology textbooks that methodically explain Christian doctrines in ways that other reformers like Philip Melanchthon or John Calvin did, Luther consistently presented the main points of the faith in well-organized works that reveal a great understanding of the faith and a unique ability to communicate theological concepts clearly. His explanation to the Apostles' Creed in the catechisms exemplifies his expertise in both theological reasoning and effective teaching.

The Lutheran reformers believed that the creeds of the church were summaries of the Bible, not additions to it. Luther even described the Apostles' Creed as "the children's creed" because of how simply it presents scriptural insights about who God is and what God does for us.[23] God creates, saves, and sustains life. Though we are not able to keep the commandments on the basis of any natural strength that belongs to us, God has not left us in our weakness. Instead, Luther wrote,

> Thus the Creed is nothing else than a response and confession of Christians based on the First Commandment. If you were to ask a young child, "My dear, what kind of God do you have? What do you know about him?" he or she could say: "First, my God is the Father, who made heaven and earth. Aside from this one alone I regard nothing as God, for there is no one else who could create heaven or earth."[24]

Though the *Large Catechism* goes on to say more about the first part of the creed, this example again shows Luther's great ability to keep things simple. Despite the endless questions that may arise about the universe and its maker, the most important thing is to know and trust that we have a good creator.

22. For instance, Gritsch, 13; and Donald McKim, ed., *The Cambridge Companion to Martin Luther* (Cambridge: Cambridge, 2003), 87 and 230.
23. Examples of Luther calling the Apostles' Creed the "Children's Creed" appear throughout this career, for instance, in LW 12:114; 13:296; 15:309; 22:24; 24:238; 41:106, 132 and 143–44. See also, SA 325 note 163.
24. LC 432.11.

While it is possible to start massive works of theology by reflecting on God and creation as taught in the first article of the creed, Reformation historian Timothy Wengert has noticed that Luther lets the creed teach us in reverse: our experience of God begins with the activity of the Holy Spirit.[25] Confronted with all kinds of ideas about who God is and how we ought to know, love, and serve God correctly, Luther taught that faith begins with the merciful work of God who comes to us first. As he wrote in his explanation to the third article of the creed (on the Holy Spirit):

> I believe that by my own understanding or strength I cannot believe in Jesus Christ my Lord or come to him, but instead the Holy Spirit has called me through the gospel, enlightened me with his gifts, made me holy and kept me in the true faith, just as he calls, gathers, enlightens, and makes holy the whole Christian church on earth and keeps it with Jesus Christ in the one common, true faith. Daily in this Christian church the Holy Spirit abundantly forgives all sins—mine and those of all believers. On the Last Day the Holy Spirit will raise me and all the dead and will give to me and all believers in Christ eternal life.[26]

Luther's view—that the Holy Spirit creates faith—turns salvation upside down. When it is up to us, we do not trust our lives to God and cannot save ourselves: we do not have the strength or ability to love God, neighbors, or self correctly. God knows this and has done something about it. Every day, one day at a time until the Last Day, the Holy Spirit calls people into faith and raises them into life with God. We experience this entirely passively: the saving actions flow in only one direction, so that the correct human response to God's grace is not activity or cooperation but sheer gratitude. Any work of ours that would put us back in the driver's seat of salvation only shows how easily we keep breaking the first commandment.

Knowing that faith comes from outside of us through the Holy Spirit, the second article of the creed presents the Christian center of who God is and what God does for us. In Jesus Christ, God gave everything—even God's very life and being—out of pure love for us.

25. Wengert, *Martin Luther's Catechisms*, 43–47 and 67.
26. LC 355–356.6.

God did not stay far away from our all-too-human weaknesses or put the burden of salvation back on us. Instead, in Christ we see the love of God for this world in the flesh. In response, Luther summarized what Christians believe and confess (*credimus et confitemur*) in the creed this way: "I believe that Jesus Christ, true God, begotten of the Father in eternity, and also a true human being, born of the Virgin Mary, is my LORD."[27]

This little sentence offers an abundance of riches about the Bible, Christian theology, and personal testimony. First, Luther's capitalization of Lord sends us back to the first two commandments, to the God of Israel, creator of heaven and earth, whose holy name is "I AM WHO I AM" (Exod 3:14). Next, Lutherans share in the New Testament witness that the Jesus of Nazareth who "was crucified, suffered, died and was buried" is one with this almighty Lord of creation. The cross of Christ is at the heart of who God is and what God does, transforming weakness, shame, and death into power, life, and blessing. This conviction about Christ's deity follows New Testament passages like Matt 8:25, Luke 24:34, Phil 2:11, and Col 1:19-20.

Further, Luther's use of "*my* Lord" also reminds us that this is not an abstract deity but one who came to redeem real people. When it comes to knowing what kind of God we have, Luther described it like this:

> [Christ] has purchased and freed me from all sins, from death, and from the power of the devil, not with gold or silver but with his holy, precious blood and with his innocent suffering and death. He has done all this in order that I may belong to him, live under him in his kingdom, and serve him in all righteousness, innocence, and blessedness, just as he is risen from the dead and lives and rules eternally.[28]

In Christ, we have a God who will do everything for us, even one who will become a curse because of love for us; we have a Lord who—though he had all divine power, righteousness, and strength—emptied himself and gave his own lifeblood so that we who are otherwise empty of these things might have the fullness of God.[29] In his words on the

---

27. SC 355.4.
28. LC 355.4.

second article, Luther compactly offers profound teachings about the Trinity, the incarnation, the cross, and atonement. What kind of God do we have? The children's creed has told us, through this summary of Christ's great mercy and self-giving love.

At this point, it is worth asking: is the central Reformation doctrine of justification by faith alone present in this important discussion? At no point did Luther interrupt his catechism to insert a separate "doctrine of justification." It turns out, however, that he did not need to. First, the creed itself clearly announces the good news of salvation through Jesus Christ alone, God's free justification of the ungodly, apart from any human works or merit. Second, Luther connected Christ's activity with the forgiveness of sins. In this way, the reformers saw the doctrine of justification also appearing in the third article's words, "I believe . . . in the forgiveness of sins." The Holy Spirit continues to lead people into life and salvation by forgiving sins freely through faith in Jesus Christ; the gospel in a nutshell.

Luther's explanation of the creed deftly weaves together the theology of the cross, justification by faith alone, and the ongoing work of the Holy Spirit who creates faith and renews human hearts. When it comes to the church's work today, Luther commended the entire mission of the church to the good guidance of the Holy Spirit:

> This, then, is the article that must always remain in force. For creation is now behind us, and redemption has also taken place, but the Holy Spirit continues its work without ceasing until the Last Day, and for this purpose has appointed a community on earth, through which the Spirit speaks and does all its work.[30]

The ongoing work of the Holy Spirit means that the faith taught in the creed is more than a body of Christian knowledge. Faith means meeting God in and through the Spirit-led work of Christ and his community, which then shares this healing word and work with the rest of creation. The Christian church exists to be this people where good news is

---

29. Gal 3:13, 2 Cor 5:21, and Phil 2:5-11.
30. LC 439.61. I have amended the language here to be gender inclusive. In German, the word for Spirit, *Geist*, is grammatically masculine, which does not imply that the Holy Spirit is male.

announced, received, and shared. In case that mission starts to sound too lofty or complicated, all of this can be learned, remembered and experienced through the children's creed.

## Prayer and Spirituality

The next section of Luther's catechisms is the Lord's Prayer, which invites us to ponder the spiritual, prayerful, meditative side of our lives as humans. What is spirituality? In one way, spirituality can seem very democratic and easily accessible, as if anyone can cultivate spirituality through prayer, meditation, or other personal spiritual practices. In another way, though, spirituality can inspire thoughts of truly holy people (spiritual mountain climbers) who ascend to high and lofty places, free from the mundane concerns of life below. Either way, we often talk about spirituality as if it is something that we humans do to get closer to God or deeper into our own spiritual lives.

Following the idea that the Holy Spirit brings spirituality to us, however, Luther's catechisms focus on experiencing spirituality in both the highs and lows of human existence. Why? Because Christ does not send us to meet him somewhere over the rainbow, far from the world as we know it. Neither does he tell us to find holiness by seeking it in ourselves. Instead, God has promised to meet us here on solid ground, as people who live in real bodies and real communities.

For this reason, major elements of Lutheran spiritual life include seemingly simple things that we have already seen at work in the catechisms. In the church's regular practice of confession and forgiveness, worshipers reflect on their lives in light of God's commandments, on those things "done and left undone" that have broken relationships with God, neighbor, creation, and self. Time for honest confession of sin in our lives sends us back to God for reconciliation with the Lord and each other. This is a deep spiritual practice rooted in the Bible, which provides a starting point for daily reflection and community life.

Lutherans also often include one of the ancient creeds, usually the Apostles' or Nicene Creed, as another spiritual practice in worship.

Sometimes this can seem to be a rote recitation of a set of abstract religious doctrines. But consider what is happening in such moments: a community once again shares—confesses—the conviction that God loves us, saves us, and sustains us. Worshipers together believe in their hearts and confess with their lips, saying, "I believe" and "we believe" in this God of grace, love, and mercy. Such a confession of faith changes one's worldview. A side benefit of confessing a creed in worship is that no matter what else one hears, sees, or thinks during worship, the good news has been announced and confessed for all to hear.

Another key part of Lutheran spiritual life is praying the Lord's Prayer (also called the Our Father), which appears in Matthew 6 and Luke 11 in two slightly different versions. Of course, Lutherans have no unique claim on this prayer. But through the catechism and its central place in worship, Martin Luther reminded people what a profound treasure and spiritual resource the church has in this little prayer.

### Why Pray?

In discussing the Lord's Prayer in the *Large Catechism*, Luther reviewed several reasons why we pray.[31] First, the commandment against taking the Lord's name in vain implies that there are right ways to call upon God's name, including prayer. Next, we pray because God has promised to listen. "God has made and affirmed a promise: that what we pray is a certain and sure thing. As he says in Psalm 50[:15], 'Call on me in the day of trouble; I will deliver you,' and as Christ says in the Gospel of Matthew 7[:7-8], 'Ask, and it will be given you.'" Third, God wants us to pray so much that Christ even gave us words to use so that we need not worry about what to say. Finally, this prayer teaches us to reflect on our real needs in life. "For we are all lacking plenty of things: all that is missing is that we do not feel or see them. God therefore wants you to lament and express your needs and concerns, not because he is unaware of them, but in order that you may kindle your heart to

31. The following paragraph is a summary of LC 441–44.

stronger and greater desires and open and spread your apron wide to receive many things."[32]

On this final point, Luther noticed that the Lord's Prayer begins with our need for God. This is remarkable because (as Albrecht Peters noted in his detailed study of the catechisms), if it were up to us, we would probably start with the petitions requesting food, forgiveness, and safety.[33] Citing Luther's short exposition of the Lord's Prayer (1519), Peters said, "Whenever we self-centered humans pray on our own accord, we start out from the very last petition" to the effect that we "therefore never penetrate to the first three petitions of the Our Father."[34] Like the first commandment, therefore, the Lord's Prayer teaches us to keep God first and to view all our prayers and needs in light of God's unfailing goodness and mercy.

Luther further explained the words about God's kingdom and God's will in such a way as to comfort Christians who may be anxious about the future.

> God's kingdom comes on its own without our prayer, but we ask in this prayer that it may also come to us. How does this come about? Answer: Whenever our heavenly Father gives us his Holy Spirit, so that through his grace we believe his Holy Word and live godly lives here in time and hereafter in eternity.[35]

God's will, God's kingdom, and God's church do not depend on us. God's kingdom will come no matter what. We respond to this promise by praying that we get to keep being a part of it! How will we know if we are participating in the kingdom of God? We will hear the word of God in our midst and see the fruits of the Holy Spirit in our daily lives. Such fruits and benefits of the Holy Spirit are worth our devout prayers, especially in times when the well-being of our lives, our communities, or our churches might seem to be in doubt.

What do we do, however, when this prayer does not seem to be

---

32. LC 444.27.
33. Albrecht Peters, *Commentary on Luther's Catechisms: Lord's Prayer*, translated by Daniel Thies (St. Louis: Concordia, 2011), 13.
34. Peters, 13.
35. SC 356–357.7-8.

answered, when hardships increase rather than decrease? On this point, the *Large Catechism* looked to the cross for encouragement:

> Therefore we who would be Christians must surely expect to have the devil with all his angels and the world as our enemies and must expect that they will inflict every possible misfortune and grief upon us. For where God's Word is preached, accepted, or believed, and bears fruits, there the holy and precious cross will also not be far behind.[36]

Far from leading us onto an easy path of holiness and righteousness, Luther believed that the more one lives in God's word, the more the devil will attack. As Heiko Oberman wrote, "In Luther's view, it is not a life dedicated to secular tasks and worldly business that attracts and is targeted by the Devil. On the contrary, where Christ is present, the adversary is never far away: 'When the Devil harasses us, then we know ourselves to be in good shape!'"[37] These attacks need not keep us from God but teach us increasingly to rely upon Christ. Lutheran spirituality thus includes a willingness to experience and redefine suffering in light of Christ's cross, which always condemns sin and promises life. In that sense, Luther's words about the Lord's Prayer provide a great example of Luther's theology of the cross—and the school of the cross—at work in the *Book of Concord*.

At the same time, suffering does not excuse those who inflict the pain; nor does it impose a burden of reconciliation or acceptance onto those who suffer unjustly. Rather, to return to the language of the *Heidelberg Disputation* cited in the previous chapter, theologians of the cross call a thing what it is: namely, sin and injustice. In faith, Christians can name and confront the hurts caused by sin, as well as claim the power of God to lift up the lowly and set captives free.

## Praying for Each Other

Turning from spiritual to physical needs, Luther interpreted the prayer for "daily bread" in a very expansive way. What is daily bread? It is:

36. LC 448–449.65.
37. Heiko Oberman, *Luther: Man between God and the Devil*, translated by Eileen Walliser-Schwarzbart (New Haven, CT: Yale, 1989), 106.

Everything included in the necessities and nourishment for our bodies, such as food, drink, clothing, shoes, house, farm, fields, livestock, money, property, an upright spouse, upright children, upright members of the household, upright and faithful rulers, good government, good weather, peace, health, decency, honor, good friends, faithful neighbors, and the like.[38]

Luther expanded the prayer for daily bread to include everything that goes into making sure food reaches our stomachs, including the social and economic worlds that we live in. Without confusing God's work with our serious efforts to foster justice on earth, Luther here expressed a clear political theology. Peace, government, and employment are all positive factors in meeting real human needs, so that those who serve these good ends are participating in God's loving work to serve and sustain creation. When it comes to this petition for daily bread, therefore, Luther wrote:

Indeed, the greatest need of all is to pray for the civil authorities and the government, for it is chiefly through them that God provides us daily bread and all the comforts of this life. Although we have received from God all good things in abundance, we cannot retain any of them or enjoy them in security and happiness were he not to give us a stable, peaceful government. For where dissension, strife, and war prevail, there daily bread is already taken away or at least reduced.

It would therefore be fitting if the coat of arms of every upright prince were emblazoned with a loaf of bread instead of a lion . . . or if a loaf of bread were stamped on coins, in order to remind both princes and subjects that it is through the princes' office that we enjoy protection and peace and that without them we could neither eat nor preserve the precious gift of bread.[39]

Similar to the themes of the fourth commandment, Luther here praised good economic order and upright government as a gift of God to such an extent that he named feeding people as the primary task of all economic and political life.[40] This does not put authority figures in the place of God but lifts them up as servants of God and of their

38. SC 357.14.
39. LC 450.74.
40. It should be noted that in this place "princes" includes other political bodies like city councils.

neighbors. Additionally, good political and business practices not only serve people in a physical sense but are also part of the holy and spiritual work of caring for creation.

This high view of servant leadership cannot be overstated. When we serve our fellow citizens by making sure that daily bread reaches real stomachs, we are participating in the fulfillment of this prayer. Helping meet basic human needs is so central to political and social life together that a loaf of bread ought to be the symbol for all our governmental offices.

Luther's teaching about this petition also included care for the environment. As he put it, the devil is against life and peace and therefore works to create disorder and social upheaval. "This is why he [the devil] causes so much contention, murder, sedition, and war, why he sends storms and hail to destroy crops and cattle, why he poisons the air, etc."[41] Because war, sedition, and "poisoned air" keep people from receiving their daily bread, we pray that we and the people around us not be damaged by such harm and neglect.

Unlike Luther, people today might not blame storms and hail on the devil. Nevertheless, as a growing body of research and literature shows, access to abundant and clean water often plays key roles in the diseases, wars and uprisings that continued to plague people.[42] Luther's words here connect respect for the environment with good public policy and the holy work of service to others. In our time, therefore, we can add those who care for the environment to the list of those who serve their neighbor by making sure that all receive their "daily bread."

The spiritual wisdom of the Lord's Prayer also positively impacts daily life through the prayer for forgiveness: "Forgive us our sins, as

---

41. LC 451.80.
42. As contributions to this important growing body of research, see, Eliza Griswold, *The Tenth Parallel: Dispatches from the Fault Line between Christianity and Islam* (New York: Farrar, Straus and Giroux, 2010); Willis Jenkins, *Ecologies of Grace: Environmental Ethics and Christian Theology* (Oxford: Oxford, 2008); Elizabeth Kolbert, *Field Notes from a Catastrophe: Man, Nature, and Climate Change* (New York: Bloomsbury, 2006); James Howard Kunstler, *The Long Emergency: Surviving the Converging Catastrophes of the Twenty-First Century* (New York: Atlantic Monthly Press, 2005); Bill McKibbon, *The End of Nature* (New York: Random House, 1989); and *An Inconvenient Truth: A Global Warming*, directed by Davis Guggenheim, starring Al Gore (Paramount, 2006), DVD.

we forgive those who sin against us." This petition signaled to the reformers that Christ had not imagined his disciples would advance into a sinless state in this life. Instead, Christ taught his followers to grow in awareness of the depth of sin throughout our days. As Luther put it, "we are not without sin," and "it is not possible always to stand firm in this ceaseless conflict [against sin]."[43] Every time Christians pray the Lord's Prayer, therefore, we include a confession of our own sin and once again commend ourselves to God's mercy.

At the same time, however, this petition can sound as if our being forgiven by God depends on our doing something first, as the words that follow this prayer in Matthew 6 further emphasize: "For if you forgive others their trespasses, your heavenly Father will also forgive you; but if you do not forgive others, neither will your heavenly Father forgive your trespasses" (Matt 6:14-15). Does our being forgiven by God depend on our prior forgiveness of others? Is salvation up to us? While recognizing Christ's instructions to forgive others, Luther interpreted the second half of the petition as a promise, not a threat:

> if you forgive, you have the comfort and assurance that you are forgiven in heaven—not on account of your forgiving (for [God] does it altogether freely, out of pure grace, because he has promised it, as the gospel teaches) but instead because he has set this up for our strengthening and assurance as a sign along with the promise that matches this petition in Luke 6[:37], "Forgive, and you will be forgiven." Therefore Christ repeats it immediately after the Lord's Prayer, saying in Matthew 6:[14], "If you forgive others their trespasses, your heavenly Father will also forgive you . . ."

> Therefore, this sign is attached to the petition so that when we pray we may recall the promise . . . For whatever baptism and the Lord's Supper, which are appointed to us as outward signs, can effect, this sign can as well, in order to strengthen and gladden our conscience. Moreover, above and beyond the other signs, it has been instituted precisely so that we can use and practice it every hour, keeping it with us at all times.[44]

In Luther's interpretation, this potentially menacing admonition to

---

43. LC 452.86 and 87.
44. LC 453.93-98. See also Peters, *Lord's Prayer*, 157.

forgive others has been transformed into a new sacrament of forgiveness that is constantly with us and ready to be put into practice. Our forgiving others is a sign, promise and reminder that God has already forgiven the ungodly freely through faith.

## Yes, Yes, It Shall Be So

In his discussion of "lead us not into temptation," Luther seemed to take a major shortcut when he wrote, "It is true that God tempts no one."[45] Luther believed that suffering, temptations and the cross always accompany faith; he also knew the many biblical stories of testing and temptation very well. So how could he seemingly minimize these words about temptation in the Lord's Prayer?

First, the phrase God "tempts no one" is a direct citation of Jas 1:13; even though it is a theological shortcut, it is at least a biblical one. Second, since the catechisms are meant to support daily faith, it makes sense that Luther would emphasize God's care for us in the midst of our lifelong struggles with sin and temptation. As the second commandment instructs, this petition sends us calling out to God alone for life and deliverance, no matter how dire our situation. Like Peter and the disciples who abandoned Christ in the time of trial, we cannot withstand trials and temptations on our own. Instead, we pray desperately to God to come to our aid and deliver us from all the evils that assail us.

Luther's conclusion to the Lord's Prayer wonderfully summarized this fundamental faith and confidence in God. "'Amen, amen' means 'Yes, yes, it is going to come about just like this.'"[46] Here again, faith fulfills the commandments to trust in God with the confident assurance that God can and will lead us into life.

The Lord's Prayer provides great spiritual wisdom and practical insight for faith and daily life. It includes discussion of central doctrines like creation and justification. It advances a practical theology that sees care for creation, food for the hungry, good

---

45. SC 358.18.
46. SC 358.21. Older translations say, "Yes, yes, it shall be so."

government, and civil peace as gifts from God. Further, it always sends us to the Lord for forgiveness, strength, freedom, and life. This little biblical prayer offers both deep spirituality and practical encouragement for our journey through life.

### The Sacraments: What They Are and What They Do

In the previous chapter, we saw that Melanchthon's 1521 *Loci Communes* not only defined theological topics but also described the effects of various teachings. Luther's explanations of the sacraments of baptism and the Lord's Supper show a clear and explicit use of this focus on both "what a thing is" and "what a thing does" (*quid sit, quid effectus*). Luther, Melanchthon and their colleagues consistently used and taught this approach.

Luther's explanation to the sacrament of baptism in the *Small Catechism* begins with the question "What is baptism?" and then follows it up by asking, "What gifts or benefits does baptism grant?"[47] The explanation to the Lord's Supper follows the same pattern, asking, "What is the Sacrament of the Altar?" followed shortly afterwards by the question, "What is the benefit of such eating and drinking?"[48] Sacraments are not merely rituals to be enacted or doctrines to be believed. Instead, they are gifts of grace, life, and forgiveness that people personally receive and benefit from.

The *Large Catechism* makes this same move from what the sacraments are to the benefits that they give. There Luther's discussion of baptism covers three main topics: what it is, what it does, and who receives it. This latter part emphasizes that faith receives the sacrament. This does not mean that the sacrament depends on right faith to be valid, but rather that faith is a relationship with God that receives and believes the promises that God gives through word and water: "faith does not make baptism; rather, it receives baptism."[49]

Because more radical reformers in the 1520s—including Luther's

---

47. SC 359.1 and 5.
48. SC 362.1 and 5.
49. LC 463.53.

former colleague Andreas Karlstadt—had started to question why infants are baptized, Luther let this third point introduce a discussion of infant baptism. For one thing, he remarked that respected Christians in centuries before him such as St. Bernard of Clairvaux had been baptized as infants. The fact that such lives revealed the work of the Holy Spirit demonstrated that their baptisms as infants had been valid.[50] The baptism of infants also emphasized that baptism is God's word and work given to us, not something that people make themselves worthy to receive.

The *Large Catechism*'s words about the Lord's Supper are even more explicit about moving from "what a thing is" to "what a thing does." There Luther began: "As we heard about Holy Baptism, so we must speak about the second sacrament in the same way, under three headings, stating what it is, what its benefits are, and who is to receive it. All this is established from the words Christ used to institute it."[51] This sentence about Christ's words grounds the use of the sacrament in the Bible. As with the other parts of the catechism, the sacraments are scripturally-based gifts, whose validity, depth and use comes not from human ideas about holiness but from the word of God.

On the point of who receives the sacrament of communion worthily, Luther spoke of his own worries on this subject and shared his personal and pastoral journey.

> But suppose you say, "What if I feel that I am unfit?" Answer: This is my struggle as well, especially inherited from the old order under the pope when we tortured ourselves to become so perfectly pure that God might not find the least blemish in us. Because of this we became so timid that everyone was thrown into consternation, saying, "Alas, you are not worthy!" Then nature and reason begin to contrast our unworthiness with this great and precious blessing, and it appears like a dark lantern in contrast to the bright sun, or as manure in contrast to jewels; then because they see this, such people will not go to the sacrament and wait until they are prepared, until one week passes into another and one half-year into yet another. If you choose to fix your eye on how good and pure you are, to wait until nothing torments you, you will never go. . . .

50. LC 462–463.50, baptism.
51. LC 467.1.

> People with such misgivings must learn that it is the highest art to realize
> that this sacrament does not depend upon our worthiness. For we are not
> baptized because we are worthy and holy, nor do we come to confession
> as if we were pure and without sin; on the contrary, we come as poor,
> miserable people, precisely because we are unworthy.[52]

Who is worthy? Those who know their need for grace. This teaching declares the personal message that the sacrament offers God-given means of grace, life, and forgiveness *for you*. Through baptism and the Lord's Supper, real sinners get to see, touch and taste God's real goodness for ourselves. We hear the divine promise attached to these elements in the words "you are baptized" and "given for you, shed for you." Looking ahead to the *Formula of Concord*, we see that this twin focus on "what a thing is" and "what a thing does" remained a hallmark of Lutheran theology and piety. Written almost fifty years after the catechisms, the *Formula of Concord* affirms that the sacrament of communion "presents Christ to us as true God and a true human being along with all his benefits (God's grace, forgiveness of sins, righteousness, and eternal life)."[53]

Luther's personal reflection about his time as a monk also invites us to see the early Reformation at work in the catechisms: looking for a gracious God, he learned to lean upon the sacraments as firm promises of grace to sinners. In this way, his words on baptism similarly resonate with Thesis 1 on repentance in the 95 *Theses* of 1517. Connecting baptism to this lifelong journey of repentance and faith, Luther wrote in the *Large Catechism*, "Thus a Christian life is nothing else than a daily baptism, begun once and continuing ever after."[54] Making the relationship between baptism and repentance even more explicit, he said:

> Here you see that baptism, both by its power and by its signification,
> comprehends also the third sacrament, formerly called penance, which
> is really nothing else than baptism. What is repentance but an earnest
> attack on the old creature and an entering into a new life? If you live

---

52. LC 472.55–473.61.
53. SD 604.62.
54. LC 465.65.

in repentance, therefore, you are walking in baptism, which not only announces this new life but also produces, begins, and exercises it. . . . Repentance, therefore, is nothing else than a return and approach to baptism, to resume and practice what has earlier been begun but abandoned.[55]

Though separated by more than a decade, here we find a close connection between the 95 Theses and the catechisms. The early Luther's world-changing call to repentance and faith found clear expression in how he taught the sacraments to pastors, parishioners, and children later in the Reformation.

The theology of the cross is also present in Luther's view of baptism as a dying and rising with Christ. Teaching the significance of baptism, he wrote, "It signifies that the old creature in us with all sins and evil desires is to be drowned and die through daily contrition and repentance, and on the other hand that daily a new person is to come forth and rise up to live before God in righteousness and purity forever."[56] Here Luther connected the benefits of baptism with the treasure of the cross. "Thus you see plainly that baptism is not a work that we do but that it is a treasure that God gives us and faith grasps, just as the Lord Christ upon the cross is not a work but a treasure placed in the setting of the Word and offered to us in the Word and received by faith."[57]

Finally, Luther discussed the radical freedom that Christians have through faith (another key theme of the early Reformation) in his passionate teaching about what baptism is and does.

Thus, we must regard baptism and put it to use in such a way that we may draw strength and comfort from it when our sins or conscience oppress us, and say: "But I am baptized! And if I have been baptized, I have the promise that I shall be saved and have eternal life, both in soul and body."[58]

55. LC 465.74–466.79.
56. SC 360.12.
57. LC 461.37.
58. LC 462.44-45.

## Conclusion

Written in the late 1520s, Luther's catechisms share much of the faith and energy that launched the Reformation a decade earlier. Although they teach many potentially abstract theological ideas (for instance, "what does it mean to have a god?"), the catechisms developed from sermons given to regular parishioners and aim to explain complicated ideas in understandable and beneficial ways. From the outset, these works also included multi-media elements like posters, pictures, and songs, so that people might come to learn in ways that made sense to them.

When speaking of the catechisms' content, it is important to remember that Luther wanted people to know the primary sources of the commandments, creed, Lord's Prayer, and sacraments themselves. Therefore, to know the catechism meant to know these biblical sources. His own comments were offered in a secondary way to help learners understand these texts better, not to supplant or overshadow the biblical material.

From spiritual insights about prayer and rising with Christ to practical matters of how Christians care for their neighbors, Luther's *Large* and *Small Catechisms* remain strong resources from the Lutheran tradition. They continue to teach what it means that the Lord who was born among us, gave his life for sinners, and rose from the dead: "He has done all this in order that I may belong to him."[59]

59. SC 355.4.

# 4

---

# The *Augsburg Confession*: Faith for a Grounded, Flexible Church

For the 1530 imperial diet in Augsburg, Holy Roman Emperor Charles V invited his protesting subjects to present a statement of their faith. Philip Melanchthon, who gave the *Augsburg Confession* most of its shape and expression, thus needed to show that Evangelical Lutheran reforms belonged solidly to the larger Christian tradition.

For this reason, the *Augsburg Confession* (also called the *Augustana* or CA, for its Latin name *Confessio Augustana*) stressed the reformers' desire to maintain unity with the universal church. At the same time, it laid out a vision of the faith, the church, and Christian life that remains distinctive among other Reformation movements, especially in how justification by faith shapes Christian living and contextual approaches to sharing the gospel. Here, too, themes of Luther's early career (including repentance, the theology of the cross, and Christian freedom) appear in clear and practical ways. Expressing the Lutherans' concern for harmony, Melanchthon wrote a prayer for an open and amicable discussion of contested issues into the *Augustana*'s preface:

Thus, the matters at issue between the parties may be presented in writing on both sides; they may be negotiated charitably and amicably; and these same differences may be so explained as to unite us in one, true religion, since we are all enlisted under one Christ and should confess Christ. All of this may be done in consequence of Your Imperial Majesty's aforementioned summons and in accord with divine truth. We, therefore, invoke God Almighty in deepest humility and pray for the gift of his divine grace to this end. Amen![1]

More than just a set of theological statements, the *Augustana* offers a prayerful statement of shared beliefs. As this excerpt shows, it was not unusual for either Luther or Melanchthon to insert prayers and invocations into their writings, as they wrote with the hope that their efforts might bear good fruit.

While there are many rich ways to read and interpret the *Augsburg Confession*, this chapter will focus on the passionate faith that it presents, as well as the effects that the Lutheran doctrine of justification has for matters of church structures and Christian living. Continuing the "what it is" and "what it does" theme discussed earlier in this book, this chapter also examines the *Augsburg Confession*'s view of who the Holy Spirit is and what the Spirit does; what the church is and what it does; what faith is and what Christian faith does.

## Lutherans and the Holy Spirit

Although there is no separate article on the Holy Spirit, the *Augsburg Confession* frequently invokes the Holy Spirit who creates faith, gives grace, and sustains the church. This view of the Holy Spirit appears at the outset, as article 1 expresses the reformers' agreement with the ancient Christian teaching of the Triune God: one God in three co-equal and co-eternal persons; God the Father, God the Son, and God the Holy Spirit.[2] In addition to Luther's discussion of the Apostles' Creed in the catechisms and the inclusion of the three ecumenical creeds with the *Book of Concord*, CA article 1 is a typical and uncontroversial Lutheran affirmation of classical Trinitarian faith.

1. CA 32.10-11.
2. CA I 36.3.

70

More than just a formal nod to orthodox Trinitarian teaching, however, the Holy Spirit continues to fill the *Augsburg Confession*, appearing in four of the first five articles. Article 2 on original sin teaches that humans are lost in sin and cannot have either true fear of God or true faith in God without being "born again through baptism and the Holy Spirit."[3] This means that the work of salvation does not begin with any work of a person's body, mind, or soul, but rather with the Holy Spirit. This resonates with Luther's words in the Small Catechism: "I believe that by my own understanding or strength I cannot believe in Jesus Christ my Lord or come to him, but instead the Holy Spirit has called me. . . ."[4]

The Holy Spirit also appears in article 3 on the Son of God. After summarizing the teaching about Jesus Christ in the Apostles' Creed, this article says that Christ "will sanctify those who believe in him by sending into their hearts the Holy Spirit, who will rule, console, and make them alive and defend them against the devil and the power of sin."[5] As we noticed in the catechism, Lutherans believe that justification is itself a Trinitarian process: the Holy Spirit of God creates faith and gives the benefits that Christ won through his death and resurrection, reconciling us with a gracious and loving Father. It is therefore no wonder that the article on the Son of God also includes the saving work of the Holy Spirit.

This Trinitarian view of justification continues in articles 4 and 5, which in Melanchthon's original text belonged to the same paragraph (the articles were numbered later). Article 4 of the *Augsburg Confession* provides the classic Lutheran statement of justification by faith. But to show how directly the work of the Holy Spirit relates to justification, articles 4 and 5 are presented here in their continuity.

3. CA II 39.2.
4. SC 355.6. It is important to note that the German word for spirit, *der Geist*, is grammatically masculine, leading to the use of the male pronoun "he" for the Spirit throughout the *Book of Concord*. In Hebrew, the word for spirit is grammatically feminine. In Greek, it is grammatically neuter. Therefore, the use of "he" should not suggest that the Lutheran reformers believed that the Holy Spirit was essentially male. Luther's definition of "what it means to have a god" in the *Large Catechism* challenges the idolatry that can come from mistaking gendered human language and gender constructs with the living God whose name is I AM WHO I AM.
5. CA III 39.5.

[Article 4] Furthermore, it is taught that we cannot obtain forgiveness of sin and righteousness before God through our merit, work, or satisfactions, but that we receive forgiveness of sin and become righteous before God out of grace for Christ's sake through faith when we believe that Christ has suffered for us and that for his sake our sin is forgiven and righteousness and eternal life are given to us. For God will regard and reckon this faith as righteousness in his sight, as St. Paul says in Romans 3[:21-26] and 4[:5]. [Article 5] To obtain such faith God instituted the office of preaching, giving the gospel and the sacraments. Through these, as through means, he gives the Holy Spirit who produces faith, where and when he wills, in those who hear the gospel. It teaches that we have a gracious God, not through our merit but through Christ's merit, when we so believe. Condemned are the Anabaptists and others who teach that we obtain the Holy Spirit without the external word of the gospel through our own preparation, thoughts, and works.[6]

While these articles will be discussed more below, we note here how the work of the Holy Spirit is essential to salvation. Jesus Christ is reconciliation and justification for all who believe; the Holy Spirit connects this divine healing with real human hearts through the embodied experiences of hearing the gospel and receiving the sacraments. That is, the ministry of the church and the office of preaching are themselves God-given ways in which the Holy Spirit continuously produces saving faith.

The condemnation of "Anabaptists and others" in article 5 (cited above) was the Lutherans' way of saying that people should not look for the Holy Spirit outside God's promises to be present in God's word, sacraments, and church. By this point in the Reformation, many people had come to believe that they could know God by spiritual revelation outside of the scriptures and the church. Lutherans as well as Roman Catholics rejected that view, affirming instead that the Holy Spirit works as promised in scripture and in the means of grace offered in worship, prayer, and community.

With articles 4 and 5 working together, we see that the Holy Spirit serves an essential and active role in the Lutheran view of who God is and what God does to save us. The Holy Spirit of God liberates people

6. CA IV and V 38.1–40.4.

from the bondage of sin (article 2) and creates saving faith in Christ through the God-given means of gospel preaching and the grace of sacraments (articles 3–5).

The *Augsburg Confession* shows a remarkable consistency in this description of the Holy Spirit. Article 18, which discusses free will, echoes the teaching on original sin, as it states, "without the grace, help, and operation of the Holy Spirit a human being cannot become pleasing to God, fear or believe in God with the whole heart, or expel innate evil lusts from the heart. Instead, this happens through the Holy Spirit, who is given through the Word of God."[7]

Regarding the faith that justifies and produces good works, CA article 20 points again to faith as the saving spiritual relationship between God and sinners. "Faith alone always takes hold of grace and forgiveness of sin. Because the Holy Spirit is given through faith, the heart is also moved to do good works. For before, because it lacks the Holy Spirit, the heart is too weak."[8] Good works follow justification; they happen because of the saving presence and activity of the Holy Spirit in the lives of believers. In this way, good gospel preaching and teaching inform not only the faith of the heart but the works of the hands. That is, preaching does not just tell people what they are supposed to do (which would simply leave people with spiritual laws and ethical rules that cannot save them) but it gives the gospel faith that fundamentally changes how we live and work in the world.

The relationship between the work of the Holy Spirit and the mission of the church appears in article 28 on bishops and church authority. When it comes to preaching and the sacraments, the Holy Spirit is both giver and gift: the Spirit creates faith through the word of God and is implanted in the hearts of believers. Through word and sacrament, Melanchthon wrote, "Not bodily but eternal things and benefits are given in this way, such as eternal righteousness, the Holy Spirit, and eternal life."[9] He then contrasted the Holy Spirit's effectiveness through preaching and the sacraments with the papal

---

7. CA XVIII 50.2–3.
8. CA XX 56.28–32.
9. CA XXVIII 92.8.

church's insistence that many other religious actions were essential for salvation. Addressing the controversial items like fasting and clerical celibacy that the reformers were challenging, Melanchthon asked, "why does divine scripture so frequently prohibit the making and keeping of human ordinances? Why does it call them teachings of the devil? Could the Holy Spirit possibly have warned against all this in vain?"[10] Throughout the *Augsburg Confession*, Melanchthon presented the conviction that the Holy Spirit works through the scriptures, gospel preaching, and the sacraments to lead people into freedom and life. This view of the Spirit's work through word and sacrament does not limit the power and work of the Holy Spirit, but rather embraces the mystery that God would do such great things through ordinary means like water, bread and wine, human preachers, and grassroots communities of faith.

## Easy as 4-5-6

### Article 4: Justification by Faith

Though it may seem surprising to many people today, the Lutheran reformers' insistence that sinners are justified by God's grace alone was entirely in agreement with the late medieval Catholic tradition, which had developed strong theologies of grace.[11] Agreeing on the total need for grace, the Lutherans differed from their Roman Catholic contemporaries in their view of *how* people receive this saving grace. For this reason, the controversial Reformation point was "justification by faith," not "justification by grace."

How do sinners receive the amazing grace that forgives sin and grants eternal life? In *The Freedom of a Christian* (among other places), Luther wrote that people receive the grace that reconciles them to God simply by trusting what God has done in Jesus Christ; that is, they receive justifying grace through faith. "This word of God cannot be received or honored in any works but must be grasped by faith

10. CA XXVIII 98.49.
11. Hamm, *The Early Luther*, 155–59 and 234–37.

alone."[12] Nearly a decade later, after having described who God is and what God has done in Jesus Christ to save sinners through the work of the Holy Spirit, CA article 4 affirmed that radical conviction of the early Luther that "we receive forgiveness of sin and become righteous before God out of grace for Christ's sake through faith."[13] Faith trusts God's promise of forgiveness through Jesus Christ and receives the promised reconciliation. No additional works of heart, mind, body, or soul are needed.

Article 4 of the *Augsburg Confession* is rightly beloved among Lutherans for providing this great statement of justification by faith. Less well known, however, articles 5 and 6 show that this doctrine of justification directly defines Lutheran views of the church's mission and works of service and love. The relationship between CA articles 4, 5, and 6 provides a great summary of a Lutheran worldview in which God's grace really changes the world.

## Article 5: Church as Means of Grace

If sinners are justified through faith, then the question becomes: how do they get this justifying faith? This is where the mission of the church begins, as article 5 says, "*So that* we may obtain this faith, the ministry of teaching the gospel and administering the sacraments was instituted."[14] Before any human actions, the Holy Spirit's work of announcing the good news of Jesus Christ already exists. The Christian church is therefore itself a means of grace, created by God to bless fallen humanity and broken lives with the gospel. It belongs to the nature of the gospel that there be an event where this divine message is proclaimed and where God-given means of grace are used and received: that holy event is called church.

But what then? Does gospel preaching remain something that only happens within worship settings or believers' private lives? Or might it affect other parts of life? Article 6 addresses this question next.

12. Luther, *The Freedom of a Christian*, 54.
13. CA IV 38.1–40.2.
14. CA V 41.1, italics added.

## Article 6: Good Trees, Good Fruit, Worthless Servants

By the time the *Augsburg Confession* was written, Lutherans had already long been accused of forbidding good works or saying that good works are not important parts of a Christian life. Against the common misconception that Lutherans then or now do not care about doing good works, CA article 6 says, "It is also taught that such faith should yield good fruit and good works and that a person must do such good works as God has commanded for God's sake but not place trust in them as if thereby to earn grace before God."[15] Here the reformers clearly affirmed how crucial it is for Christians to do good works of faith that serve neighbors and communities with no strings attached. More than just announcing a set of pious ideas, the gospel changes human hearts, which then changes behaviors, which then changes the world through acts of love. In short, the gospel brings good news and loving actions to a hurting world.

Two New Testament references arise here that help explain what the reformers meant by good works. First, as Luther did in *The Freedom of a Christian*,[16] the *Augsburg Confession* borrows the "good tree/good fruits" metaphor of Matt 7:17 and 12:33 to connect faith with good works, confident that "this faith is bound to yield good fruits."[17] Faith and good works belong to each other just like fruit naturally grows from a healthy tree. These good works of faith do not cause justification but are effects of God's love for us.

This organic connection first frees people from the burden of setting things right ourselves before God will love us; it then sends us out to serve others as Christ served us, selflessly and freely, without needing to worry about the worthiness of the people serving or being served. Having become "good trees" through faith, believers will naturally bear good fruit. They do not even need to worry about what the fruits of faith will be exactly: good works will just happen, because God has made the tree good.

---

15. CA VI 40.1-2.
16. Luther, *The Freedom of a Christian*, 75–76.
17. CA VI 41.1.

The second New Testament text used to describe the Lutheran view of good works is almost comical in its humility. Melanchthon could have cited numerous passages rewarding good works, such as "well done, good and faithful servant . . . enter into the joy of your master" (Matt 25:21) or "I have fought the good fight, I have finished the race, I have kept the faith" (2 Tim 4:7). Instead, CA article 6 cites Luke 17, in which Jesus talked about *not* rewarding servants for doing what they were supposed to do in the first place: "Do you thank the slave for doing what was commanded? So you also, when you have done all that you were ordered to do, say, 'We are worthless slaves; we have done only what we ought to have done!'"[18]

Luke 17 provides a key passages for understanding Lutheran views of good works: Lutherans know that good works belong so naturally to a justified Christian life that they are not even worth rewarding. "We have only done what we ought to have done." Nevertheless, the humble attitude towards good works does not change the fact that good works happen and always ought to happen. Like the use of the law with respect to the Ten Commandments, an absence of good works in a Christian life should become a reason to repent and turn back to God. Where good works are present, however, Christians can give thanks to God for simply participating in such blessings.

This connection between faith and good works is so important that it was repeated in CA article 20. In fact, the crucial emphasis on the right relationship between faith and good works serves as the only place in the *Augustana* where the phrase "faith alone" appears. Whenever the reformers talked about the importance of good works, they also made sure to affirm that faith alone justifies. In CA article 6, "faith alone" appears in a citation from St. Ambrose about justification.[19] In article 20, "faith alone" appears three times, as Melanchthon balanced the critique that Lutherans denied good works with a continued defense of

---

18. Luke 17:9-10, cited in CA VI 40.2.
19. CA VI 40.3 and note 51, which states that this was actually a citation of a writing that had long been falsely attributed to Ambrose, although few in the sixteenth century doubted that attribution. Nevertheless, the presence of "faith alone" in this and other venerable writings of the early church were important for Lutherans to show that they had not invented "faith alone" as a new concept.

justification by faith alone. To this end, he repeated the progression of articles 4, 5, and 6, moving from faith to the proclamation of the gospel and its natural result in good works:

> Faith alone always takes hold of grace and forgiveness of sin. Because the Holy Spirit is given through faith, the heart is also moved to do good works. For before, because it lacks the Holy Spirit, the heart is too weak . . .

> That is why this teaching concerning faith is not to be censured for prohibiting good works. On the contrary, it should be praised for teaching the performance of good works and for offering help as to how they may be done. For without faith and without Christ human nature and human power are much too weak to do good works: such as to call on God, to have patience in suffering, to love the neighbor, to engage diligently in legitimate callings, to be obedient, to avoid evil lust, etc. Such lofty and genuine works cannot be done without the help of Christ, as he himself says in John 15[:5], "Apart from me you can do nothing."[20]

Taken together, articles 4, 5, and 6 intimately bind saving faith, liberating preaching and works of service. Sinners are justified through faith in Christ. The Holy Spirit gives this saving faith through the preaching of the gospel, which is the church's reason for being. As a result of the Holy Spirit's effective work, otherwise broken people now do what they were created to do in the first place: freely and joyfully honor God and love their neighbors. What other mission does a church need than to announce and live out this message?

## God's Eternal and Adaptable Church

As we have seen, article 5 describes the church as the means through which the divine message of justification reaches human hearts and leads to good works of faith. This sense of effective mission also undergirds Melanchthon's definition of the church in articles 7 and 8, which describe what the church is and what it does.

First, the church is eternal and eternally united in Christ. Article 7 begins with the reformers affirming "that one holy church will remain forever."[21] Amid past and present anxieties about the health, unity

---

20. CA XX 56.28-29, 35-39.

and future of Christ's church, this is a profound statement of trust. With the creeds, the *Augsburg Confession* reminds us that the unity and perseverance of the church is itself an article of faith: we believe there is such a thing as God's church and its message of grace, even when it is not always easy to see.

This confidence in the eternal unity and mission of the church also recalls Luther's words on the Lord's Prayer: "In fact, God's kingdom comes on its own without our prayer, but we ask in this prayer that it may also come to us."[22] Different movements and groups come and go, but the one church of God cannot die; as Christ promised in Matt 16:18, the gates of hell will not prevail against it. Still, in light of the many ups and downs that Christian communities experience, it is good to pray that we keep getting to be a part of it.

But what is a church? Is it a human institution or a clearly defined group of people? Or is it so mystical as to be impossible to describe? Defining the church in a few words, the *Augustana* says, "The church is the assembly of saints in which the gospel is taught purely and the sacraments are administered rightly."[23] Having first defined what the church is ("the assembly of saints"), Melanchthon again moves to what it does. Church happens. The good news of Jesus Christ is announced and the sacraments are used. Real flesh-and-blood people are baptized into the bodily death and resurrection of Christ. Real sinners gather together to share the meal that Christ gave so graciously to his frightened disciples on that night he was betrayed (1 Cor 11:23). The Holy Spirit speaks to hearts through human words shared in the readings, songs, creeds, sermons, prayers and worship of the church. When people come together to share the gospel and the means of grace, then there is church. To say it another way, "Church is not a noun; it is a verb, an event . . . a happening."[24]

This "word and sacrament ministry" (as Lutherans often describe it)

21. CA VII 43.1.
22. SC 356.7.
23. CA VII 43.1.
24. Gordon Lathrop and Timothy Wengert, *Christian Assembly: Marks of the Church in a Pluralistic Age* (Minneapolis: Fortress, 2004), 27.

contains many rich spiritual practices. People gather to pray, sing, and reflect together, sometimes using ancient forms and sometimes using words, expressions and music unique to that particular community. People read and meditate upon sacred texts together. In the church event, God creates a new community in which the only spiritual status anyone has to boast about is the one given in baptism: "child of God." Further, instead of excluding those outside the community, believers learn to see a broken world through the cross: as God's beloved creation, worth giving everything for. Thus baptism gives a commission to love the world rather than escape it. If these spiritual practices and convictions sound common to many branches of Christianity, then that is the point. This shared unity, faith, and commitment to others is precisely what the Lutheran reformers meant to stress at the 1530 diet of Augsburg.

With its description of the church as an event centered on word and sacrament, the *Augsburg Confession* also allows for much flexibility in worship and community life. In its historical context, this freedom to adapt the church in ways that best serve local faith communities formed the basis for the Lutheran appeal to the pope and the emperor to tolerate their reforms. As article 7 says, "it is enough for the true unity of the church to agree concerning the teaching of the gospel and the administration of the sacraments. It is not necessary that human traditions, rites, or ceremonies instituted by human beings be alike everywhere."[25] Instead of claiming independence from the Church of Rome, the Lutherans sought to affirm basic Christian unity across differences in practice.

Melanchthon further invoked a long Christian tradition of tolerance for different local customs, as he cited the second-century bishop Iranaeus of Lyons: "Diversity in fasting does not dissolve unity in faith."[26] Throughout the *Augustana*, Melanchthon emphasized that the church exists not to enshrine particular customs but to preach the gospel and deliver its benefits to people inside and outside the church,

25. CA VIII 43.2-3.
26. CA XXVI 80.44.

all around the world. In today's diverse global contexts, this perspective continues to provide good foundations for ecumenical dialogue and for engaging local cultures, customs, and circumstances in meaningful ways.

## A Church under the Cross

At this point, we should remember that the evangelical party—both politicians and theologians—were putting their lives on the line by making this confession of faith in Augsburg. They remained in violation of the imperial Edict of Worms and the pope's excommunication of Luther; both of those documents included condemnation of those who protected or agreed with the reformer.[27] Despite these threats from the highest levels, "the princes stated that they would rather let their heads be cut off than deny their faith."[28] They were all in a very vulnerable position. The presentation of the *Augsburg Confession* itself bears witness to the theology of the cross, in which the power of God is revealed in weakness, suffering, and humiliation.

Article 20 emphasizes faith's role in making bold stands like this, as it says that without faith human nature does not "call upon God, expect anything from God, or bear the cross, but seeks and trusts in human help."[29] In this way, the theology of the cross is not an escape from the troubles, trials, and tribulations of the world but an immersion into such things.

This cross-shaped worldview is again invoked in article 26 on foods. There, defending evangelical reforms of fasting and other forms of spiritual discipline, the Lutherans asserted that their objections to fasting did not come from laziness or an unwillingness to suffer. "For concerning the cross they have always taught that Christians should

---

27. Brecht, *Martin Luther: His Road to Reformation 1483-1521*, 427.
28. Robert Kolb, *Confessing the Faith: Reformers Define the Church* (St. Louis: Concordia, 1991), 46. Kolb points out that this statement was made by one of the evangelical princes, George of Brandenburg-Ansbach, and later extended to refer to the attitude of all of the gathered Lutheran princes.
29. CA XX 57.37.

endure afflictions. To be disciplined by various afflictions and crucified with Christ is a true and serious, not a simulated, mortification [of the flesh]."[30] As taught by the early Luther and as visible in the daily dying and rising of baptismal life commended in the *Small Catechism*, the *Augsburg Confession* presents Christian life as a journey through repentance, suffering, and death into the life of God.

Because the theology of the cross stands at the heart of the *Augustana*'s view of the Christian life, we can speak of an "ecclesiology of the cross" in the Lutheran tradition. The cross does not tell people already suffering from sin that they need to keep suffering out of some mistaken sense of piety or to appease an angry God. Instead, the cross announces God's condemnation of sin, defeats the power of sin, sets captives free, and gives the weary rest. As a community centered on the cross, the church is a people among whom the truth about sin is honestly spoken (including sin within and among Christian communities), the power of God for life is joyfully announced, and the fruits of faith are cultivated and shared freely.

## Three Estates, One Calling

Churches devoted to this teaching and practice often do not look flashy or impressive in the eyes of others. Rather than seeking spiritual heights, their good works aim to serve people in the basic, routine ways that surround us every day. In the previous chapter, we encountered this view in Luther's explanation of the fourth commandment. Similarly contrasting this down-to-earth service with the lofty vows and spiritual perfection of monasticism prevalent at that time, the *Augsburg Confession* says:

> the precepts of God and true worship of God are obscured when people hear that only monks are in a state of perfection. For Christian perfection means earnestly to fear God and, at the same time, to have great faith and to trust that we have a gracious God on account of Christ; to ask for and to expect with certainty help from God in all things that are to be borne in

30. CA XXVI 79.31-32.

connection with our calling; and, in the meantime, diligently to do good works for others and to serve in our calling.[31]

The Christian life is defined by faith in God, daily calling upon the Lord for all help, and serving others in whatever situations we are in. This may not be flashy or exciting; in fact, it may be the exact opposite of flashy and exciting. Nevertheless, the *Augustana* honors such humble faith and service with the name of "Christian perfection."

This reformation of spiritual ministries and the affirmation of a "priesthood of all the baptized" was a key theme in Luther's early writings, especially in his 1520 tract *To the Christian Nobility of the German Nation*. As Timothy Wengert has shown, the "priesthood of all the baptized" lifts up a single category of Christian (namely, the baptized) without suggesting that all Christians ought to or are able to do the same work. In Lutheran churches, the call to a church vocation is a call to serve the gospel. This does not separate pastors and other church workers from other Christians. Instead, it is simply another way to serve the church and the world, just as people who work outside of church settings equally serve God and neighbors through their own particular gifts, callings, and service in other fields.[32]

As we saw above in articles 5, 7, and 8, the *Augsburg Confession* lifts up the office of ministry as the task of delivering the gospel. Article 14 similarly says that ministers should be "properly called" in such a way as to promote and demonstrate accountability to the gospel and to local congregations.[33] Beyond that, highlighting the godly service that all people do when they care for their neighbors through their daily work, Melanchthon wrote:

> It was also said that one could obtain more merit through the monastic life than through all other walks of life, which had been ordered by God, such as the office of pastor or preacher, the office of ruler, prince, lord, and the like. (These all serve in their vocations according to God's command, Word, and mandate without any contrived spiritual status).[34]

---

31. CA XXVII 89.49.
32. Timothy Wengert, *Priesthood, Pastors, Bishops: Public Ministry for the Reformation and Today* (Minneapolis: Fortress, 2008), especially its first two chapters, which are available online at: http://www.valpo.edu/ils/assets/pdfs/05_wengert.pdf.
33. CA XIV 47.

This discussion of various "walks of life"[35] as equal ways to serve continues the thought of the early Luther. It builds on the notion of "three estates" of church, family, and government that Luther developed in many places, including his *Confession Concerning Christ's Supper* (1528). There, in contrast to the idea that monastic or priestly vocations were spiritually higher than other callings, Luther explained:

> But the holy orders and true religious institutions established by God are these three: the office of priest, the estate of marriage, the civil government. All who are engaged in the clerical office or ministry of the Word are in a holy, proper, good, and God-pleasing office or order and estate . . .

> Again, all fathers and mothers who regulate their household wisely and bring up their children to the service of God are engaged in pure holiness, in a holy work and a holy order . . .

> Moreover, princes and lords, judges, civil officers, state officials, notaries, male and female servants and all who serve such persons, and further, all their obedient subjects—all are engaged in pure holiness and leading a holy life before God. For these three religious institutions or orders are found in God's Word and commandment . . .

> Above these three institutions and orders is the common order of Christian love, in which one serves not only the three orders, but also serves every needy person in general with all kinds of benevolent deeds, such as feeding the hungry, giving drink to the thirsty, forgiving enemies, praying for all men on earth, suffering all kinds of evil on earth, etc. Behold, all of these are called good and holy works. However, none of these orders is a means of salvation. There remains only one way above them all . . . faith in Jesus Christ.[36]

This passage shows the Lutheran conviction that Christian service means caring for the people around us in whatever ways God has given us: as leaders and followers, servants and masters, children and parents, pastors and parishioners, teachers and learners. Further, Christians share a common call to care to love all people and especially to serve those in need. Finally, we see once again that this service takes

34. CA XXVII 82.13.
35. "Walks of life" translates the Latin *officia* and the German *Stände*, meaning standings or statuses.
36. LW 37:364–65.

place under the cross, since "suffering all kinds of evil on earth" for the sake of others belongs to what it means to follow the crucified and risen Christ in faith.

## Civil Disobedience

As discussed above and in the previous chapter, living under the cross does not mean having a servile attitude with respect to injustice, tyranny, or abuse. Written to explain Lutheran resistance to pope and emperor, the *Augsburg Confession* itself stands as a bold statement against political and religious abuses. Further, Lutheran theology does not justify or excuse the abuse of authority; an affirmation of Rom 13:1 ("Let every person be subject to the governing authorities") does not necessarily result in a quietist or passive political theology.

For instance, the *Augsburg Confession* paraphrases Romans 13 in its teaching on civil authority (article 16) as it separates earthly politics from the spiritual kingdom of God. At the same time, however, this same article invokes Peter and John's words before the council in Acts 5:29: "We must obey God rather than any human authority."[37] The first commandment comes first. While Christians can and should live according to the laws of the land for the sake of peace and order, this does not mean thoughtlessly obeying unjust rulers and systems.

This dialectical (conversation-based) political theology reappears near the end of the *Augustana*, as Melanchthon again recalled the apostles Peter and John in a final appeal for tolerance from church and state authorities.

Our churches do not desire that the bishops restore peace and unity at the expense of their honor and dignity (even though it is incumbent on the bishops to do this, too, in an emergency). They ask only that the bishops relax certain unreasonable burdens which did not exist in the church in former times and which were adopted contrary to the custom of the universal Christian church . . . For many ordinances devised by human beings have fallen into disuse with the passing of time and need not be observed, as papal law itself testifies. If, however, this is impossible and permission cannot be obtained from them to moderate and abrogate

37. CA XVI 48.1–50.7.

such human ordinances as cannot be observed without sin, then we must follow the apostolic rule which commands us to obey God rather than any human beings [Acts 5:29].[38]

Striving for peace and unity, Lutherans requested permission to carry out their reform programs. These reforms included theological and social values like the freedom to preach justification by faith alone, the ability to reform worship and sacramental practices as best seen fit for local communities, and allowing clergy to marry. Although they were willing to negotiate on the details and discuss possible solutions, their consciences would not allow them to tolerate blanket prohibitions against reforms like these that they believed to be so thoroughly rooted in scripture.

## Conclusion

Much more could be said about the history, theology, and significance of the *Augsburg Confession*. For this study, however, it is enough to show that, at Augsburg, the evangelical party presented a confession of faith centered on God's work to save. Grounded in this free salvation, Lutherans pointed to the practical consequences of their reforms, including the view of good works as the natural fruits of faith, the flexibility that comes from believing that the gospel alone establishes church unity, and the social good that comes from encouraging all people to live out their baptisms by serving others in whatever positions they are in. Still cherished by Lutherans around the world today, the *Augsburg Confession* continues to offer a communal testimony of "here we stand."

38. CA XXVIII 102.71-75.

5

———

# Personal Faith and Shared Mission
# in the *Apology*

## Heart and Mind in the *Apology*

In a document that has come to be called the Roman Confutation, political and ecclesiastical authorities loyal to the pope rejected the ecumenically-oriented *Augsburg Confession* near the end of the summer 1530. In response, Philip Melanchthon wrote the *Apology of the Augsburg Confession* to defend the CA and to protest its rejection. He wanted to show beyond a doubt that the reformers' message—God's justification of the ungodly through faith alone in Christ alone—had deep scriptural roots and was faithful to the Christian tradition. Melanchthon also connected theology with the effects of Lutheran teachings, returning frequently to the relationship between faith, love, and good works. If Luther's early theology commended a theology of the cross, Melanchthon's work in the *Apology* similarly emphasized an ecclesiology of the cross, in which the church finds its life and mission not in its own strength or purity but in the self-giving love of Christ.

Recalling that Melanchthon has been blamed by some for having taken the life out of Luther's passionate theology (as discussed in chapter 2), this chapter challenges that idea by reading the *Apology* as a profoundly spiritual, gospel-centered testimony. This approach is relatively novel, as most people read the *Apology* for its doctrine of justification and as an intellectual defense of the *Augsburg Confession*. Such interpretations are well founded because Melanchthon wrote the articles of the *Apology* according to the classical rhetorical model of *genus iudicale*, in which a presenter advances a rational positive argument for the desired position while also refuting likely objections.[1]

At the same time, Melanchthon's careful defense of Lutheran teaching did not mean that he was engaged in a purely intellectual exercise. Throughout its pages, the *Apology* remained concerned with the spiritual, personal, and communal effects of its doctrines. As scholar Birgit Stolt has demonstrated, Luther and his colleagues did not separate intellect and emotions; rather, both resided together in the human heart. Luther "lived in an era before the Enlightenment; he shared, along with Augustine, the anthropology of the Bible, according to which the mind's organ for knowing is the heart, as the innermost center of human personality, separated from external influence and visible only to God. Heart and mind are inseparably joined to one another."[2]

What Stolt has written about the role of the heart in Luther's theology fits with Melanchthon's method of holding together definitions and effects; the concepts of "what a thing is" and "what a thing does" serve each other holistically. In this light, Melanchthon need not be understood as a cold rationalist: his way of doing theology always included a focus on embodied lives, experiences, and consequences. While readers will continue to benefit from the careful theological work that Melanchthon did in the *Apology of the Augsburg Confession*, this chapter will focus on it as a spiritual work, one which balances heart and mind.

This approach has its basis in the text itself. Melanchthon's preface

---

1. Charles Arand, "Melanchthon's Rhetorical Argument for sola fide in the Apology" in *Lutheran Quarterly* 14, 3 (Autumn 2000): 287.
2. Birgit Stolt, "Luther's Translation of the Bible," *Lutheran Quarterly* 28, 4 (Winter 2014): 373–74.

reminds us that he wrote the *Apology* as a response to the Roman Confutation that Emperor Charles V accepted at the diet of Augsburg. Since Charles himself did not want to hear any further defense of Lutheran teachings, Melanchthon decided to take the debate to the public. At the same time, he still hoped that harmony might come through honest deliberations and he renounced any desire for discord. Describing the life-and-death nature of these debates, he wrote:

> In these controversies I have always made it a point to adhere as closely as possible to traditional doctrinal formulations in order to promote the attainment of concord. I am doing much the same thing here, even though I could lead our contemporaries still further from the opponents' position. But the opponents show by their actions that they care for neither truth nor concord; they want only our blood.[3]

Presenting the benefits of evangelical reforms, Melanchthon wrote that the Lutherans had "brought to light many topics of Christian teaching that the church desperately needs." Whatever his adversaries' response would be, however, he commended the cause to Christ with a prayer: "We pray that he will help his afflicted and scattered churches and restore them to godly and lasting concord."[4] Far more was at stake for Melanchthon than theological formulations: hearts, minds, bodies, and souls were on the line. With this impassioned reason for writing stated in the preface, the *Apology* then makes its holistic case.

## Original Sin: Disease and Cure

Because the *Apology* responded to the Confutation that had been prepared by Cardinal Campeggio, Eck, Cochlaeus, and others, its outline follows the articles of the *Augustana* and the corresponding objections of the Roman Church. The first objection in the Confutation had to do with the Lutheran view of original sin (CA article 2). For most medieval Catholic thinkers, original sin was the "spark" of sin that came with being born in a fallen world. Baptism removed the guilt

3. Ap 110.11-2.
4. Ap 110.17 and 11.19.

of this sin, leaving it up to individuals to keep this spark from further leading to sinful actions; Christians who sin after baptism then need the sacrament of penance to atone for their wrongs.

Luther's theology of baptism had led to the contrasting view that original sin was not just a "spark" or tendency to sin. Original sin means entering the world with an innate lack of original righteousness. As the *Apology* puts it, this means "being ignorant of God, despising God, lacking fear and confidence in God, hating the judgment of God, fleeing this judging God, being angry with God, despairing of his grace, and placing confidence in temporal things, etc."[5] For the Lutheran reformers, this described the basic condition of human beings in this world we are all born into. With baptism, however, God redefines and recreates people, no longer seeing them in terms of their sin or what they lack but rather in terms of a grace freely given, a righteousness that comes not from the individual but from Christ.

For this reason, the Lutheran expression that Christians are simultaneously righteous and sinners (*simul iustus et peccator*) does not mean that people are part sinful and part holy. It means that people remain entirely sinful during this life according to our broken nature; at the same time (*simul*), God simultaneously declares such fallen creatures to be entirely holy and righteous. This view of original sin and Christ's righteousness appeared as early as Luther's 1515–16 *Lectures on Romans*; it remained a major point of division between Lutheran and Roman Catholic theology throughout the Reformation.[6]

When Melanchthon addressed this theme in the *Apology*, he expressed the same perspective as the early Luther. Melanchthon even included some of that recent history by citing the papal bull of excommunication against Luther, saying, "Here the opponents lash out at Luther, who wrote that 'original sin remains after baptism.'"[7] Confronting objections to the reformers' teaching, he examined the problem of original sin in light of God's solution to it. Although sin remains with us as long as we live as part of what it means to be born

5. Ap 113.8.
6. LW 25:336.
7. Ap 117.35, and note 33.

into a fallen world, God has acted through baptism and other means of grace to pour forgiveness, righteousness, and holiness into the lives of those who cannot save themselves.

This theology asks deeply personal things of believers. First, people admit that they are unable to justify themselves before God; next, they trust their entire lives to the promise that God loves them out of pure grace. The Lutheran view of original sin turns the correct diagnosis of the fallen human condition into the beginning of healing: first we admit that we have a problem; then we turn to the only one who can help us.

This idea may sound similar to the first step of Alcoholics Anonymous. Without making a direct correlation, it is worth noting that Dr. Franklin Buchman, who had a role in the founding of Alcoholics Anonymous, began his career as a Lutheran pastor.[8] As in the twelve-steps, the first step to recovery from sin is admitting that we have a problem. As Melanchthon put it in the *Apology*, "Knowledge of original sin is a necessity. For we cannot know the magnitude of Christ's grace unless we first recognize our malady."[9] Melanchthon reminded his readers that the point of this teaching is not to wallow in self-pity or feelings of powerlessness but to lead people to the "benefits of Christ," which "cannot be recognized unless we understand our evil."[10] Receiving these benefits then arises as the topic of article four, on justification by faith alone.

## Justification by Faith Alone

If original sin is the disease, what is the cure? Following the scripture and the creeds, the cure for human unrighteousness is the righteousness of God given freely through Christ. On that point, Lutherans and Catholics whole-heartedly agreed. Different views of how sinners receive the mercy and righteousness of God, however, grew into the hotly contested debate over justification.

8. Garth Lean, *Frank Buchman: A Life* (London: Constable, 1985), 16–18 and 151–53; available online: www.frankbuchman.info.
9. Ap 117.33.
10. Ap 120.50.

Of all the treatments of this key Reformation doctrine, Melanchthon's discussion of justification in article 4 of the *Apology* stands among the greatest. In it, he defined the issue as centering on the work, glory, and benefits of Christ. Because this section explains what justification is, how it is given, and what benefits it gives, Melanchthon discussed the *Augsburg Confession*'s articles 4, 5 and 6 together in this single place. He also addressed potential objections to justification by faith alone: for instance, he carefully examined contrasting views that people are justified through love or good works. This required tackling important biblical passages like 1 Cor 13:13 ("faith, hope, and love abide, these three; and the greatest of these is love") and Jas 2:24 ("a person is justified by works and not by faith alone"). With such a broad set of goals, Melanchthon's entire argument masterfully brought together many complex theological insights and remains worthy of close and careful reading today.

For all of its careful theological work, the *Apology* also speaks to hearts and hands, in addition to minds. Here Melanchthon showed the spiritual and ethical sides of Lutheran theology in action, not only in individual lives but in communal relationships. The "personal faith" that Melanchthon described in the following excerpt, for instance, has almost nothing to do with the thoughts, actions or feelings of isolated individuals; instead, it pushes people out of themselves and into the personal and embodied embrace of a merciful God. He wrote,

> And since the promise [of reconciliation with God] cannot be grasped in any other way than by faith, the gospel (which is, strictly speaking, the promise of the forgiveness of sins and justification on account of Christ) proclaims the righteousness of faith in Christ, which the law does not teach . . . This faith does not bring to God trust in our own merits, but only trust in the promise or the mercy promised in Christ.
>
> Therefore it follows that personal faith—by which an individual believes that his or her sins are remitted on account of Christ and that God is reconciled and gracious on account of Christ—receives the forgiveness of sins and justifies us. Because in repentance, that is, in terrors, faith consoles and uplifts hearts, it regenerates us and brings the Holy Spirit that we might then be able to live according to the law of God, namely, to love God, truly to fear God, truly to assert that God hears prayer, to obey

God in all afflictions, and to mortify concupiscence, etc. Thus because faith, which freely receives the forgiveness of sins, sets against the wrath of God Christ as the mediator and proprietor, it does not offer up our merits or our love. This faith is the true knowledge of Christ; it uses the benefits of Christ, it renews hearts, and it precedes our fulfillment of the law.[11]

Readers might want to examine these rich sentences and ideas more than once. They express the distinction between law and gospel, the theology of the cross, the righteousness of God given by the Holy Spirit through faith in Christ, and the experience of benefits that come to believers through "personal faith"—benefits that include love, prayer, forgiveness, endurance, freedom, renewal, and good works.

In the *Apology*, as in the Lutheran tradition more broadly, "personal" describes an individual's real experience of grace, without this experience being subjective, isolated, or up to individuals to create themselves. The spiritual benefits of faith come from outside the believer and are passively—but truly and personally—received through faith. Faith accepts what God is already promising and giving. No additional external works or inward disposition are necessary for this promise to become real in a person's life.

And yet, justification by faith alone does not mean the end of love or good works but a new beginning of love and service as the effects of justification. "Therefore, after we have been justified and reborn by faith, we begin to fear and love God . . . We also begin to love our neighbor because our hearts have spiritual and holy impulses."[12] Addressing the already frequent critique that the Lutheran emphasis on faith means indifference to good works, Melanchthon wrote that the evangelicals teach people to do good works and trust the Holy Spirit to make these works happen. "We openly confess, therefore, that the keeping of the law must begin in us and then increase more and more. And we include both simultaneously, namely, the inner spiritual impulses and the outward good works." Further, because humans cannot resist the devil to serve God and neighbor on their own, "we

11. Ap 127.43-46.
12. Ap 140.125.

pray for the Holy Spirit to govern and defend us so that we may neither be deceived and thus err nor be driven to undertake anything against God's will."[13]

This teaching lifts up both internal spirituality and outward good works, trusting and praying that the Holy Spirit will make good things happen in our otherwise fallen lives. Even so, inward piety and external works are neither conditions for receiving God's love nor good deeds that people generate in themselves; they come from God alone. Should believers be fortunate enough to see these fruits of faith in their lives, then the response is not one of pride or self-satisfaction but one of gratitude. As in the *Augsburg Confession*, Melanchthon concluded a discussion of good works by citing Luke 17:10: "When you have done all that you were ordered to do, say, 'We are worthless slaves.'"[14] Having already received fullness of life through faith, such humility is not pious pretending but an honest and grateful recognition of God's goodness.

Contrasting the harmony and service that come through faith with the strife that comes when people set themselves up as rulers and judges over others, Melanchthon discussed the meaning of Christian perfection.

> On the contrary, perfection (that is, the integrity of the church) is preserved when the strong bear with the weak, when people put the best construction on the faults of their teachers, and when the bishops make some allowances for the weakness of their people. The books of all the wise are all filled with these instructions about fairness [*aequitas*] and how in everyday life we should make many allowances for the sake of mutual peace.[15]

Christian perfection does not mean removal from the messy lives of ourselves or others; instead, it means practicing love and tolerance precisely in such challenging environments. Nothing less than "the integrity of the church" is at stake when it comes to engaging hard situations in life. This idea of fairness or equity [*aequitas*] says that both

13. Ap 142.136 and 139.
14. Ap 167.
15. Ap 155.234–156.235.

94

those who lead and those who follow should regard each other with generosity and mercy. Recalling Luther's explanation of the eighth commandment in the *Small Catechism*, Melanchthon described Christian perfection as something that happens "when people put the best construction" on the words and actions of others.

We could continue to study the *Apology*'s rich treatment of justification by faith alone much more. For now, though, it is enough that we have begun to see to how this key Reformation teaching balanced doctrinal debates with spiritual care for hearts, bodies, souls and communities.

## "An Association of Faith and the Holy Spirit"

In his book *The Early Luther: Stages in a Reformation Reorientation*, historian Berndt Hamm described a twist given to medieval mysticism by Luther's emphasis on justification by faith. Where medieval mysticism focused on unity with God through love, Luther experienced heaven being opened to him through his new understanding of Rom 1:17: "the righteous shall live by faith." As Hamm described it, "When Luther transformed the immediacy of traditional mysticism into an immediacy of the word, faith simultaneously became the central concept of the Christian life for him: faith is the confident reception of the gospel . . . In Luther, the medieval 'love mysticism' became the Reformation's 'faith mysticism.'"[16] According to Hamm, Luther had experienced God's love mystically coming to him from beyond himself. Through that experience, he came to view justification as an external spiritual truth about God which did not depend on him in the slightest: he would receive justification not because of who he was but because of who God is. At the same time, the personal experience of that entirely external gift of reconciling love became a profound spiritual reality in him.

To extend this "faith mysticism" to Melanchthon's words about the church adds a communal dimension to what it means for individuals

---

16. Hamm, *The Early Luther*, 214. See also LW 54:193–94 (table talk no. 3232c).

to be justified by faith. Repeating the *Augsburg Confession*'s definition of the church as an "assembly of believers," Melanchthon went on to describe what that means practically and spiritually. While it is true that visible signs like reading the Bible, using the sacraments and confessing the faith are part of what define a church, Melanchthon further explained, "However, the church is not only an association of external ties and rites like other civic organizations, but it is principally an association of faith and the Holy Spirit in the hearts of persons."[17]

Here Melanchthon provided a remarkably mystical, personal, and communal definition of the church. Based on this description, a local congregation might be called "A Neighborhood Association of Faith and the Holy Spirit in the Hearts of Persons." This mystical definition of the church does not remove people from real-world communities but embeds us in them even more. The "external marks" of the church (like preaching, using the sacraments, praying together, and so on) provide tangible evidence that a person really is in a Christian church. A person can trust that church is happening when they enter an assembly, hear the announcement of God's word through Bible readings, songs, liturgy, sermons, and prayers, and see that the sacraments of the church are being used in a way consistent with the New Testament and the practice of Christians across the centuries. The outward actions that happen in church are signs of the inward spiritual reality. Also, regardless of the holiness (or possible lack thereof) among the people gathered together, such outward signs retain value on their own, because they belong to God, not to people. These "marks of the church" reveal that church is happening.

Even as they cherished these outward marks of the church, the Lutheran reformers emphasized the internal change that happens through worship. United in the gospel, the kingdom of God truly is at hand. This kingdom cannot be codified or controlled by people. This is the kingdom of God, which—as Jesus said—"is not of this world" (John 18:36). As Melanchthon put it: "the kingdom of Christ is the

17. Ap 174.5.

righteousness of the heart and the gift of the Holy Spirit."[18] Institutional churches and church leaders serve as earthly stewards of this heavenly kingdom, while God remains Lord of the church. This outlook balances appreciation for good institutional structures and servant leaders with the recognition that God alone creates and sustains the church. Putting this all together, the Lutheran Confessions thus present the church as a sublime mystical body and heavenly kingdom that also can be known, seen, experienced and shepherded in down-to-earth ways. "Faith mysticism" is a good way to describe this shared life of faith in the Lutheran tradition.

This does not mean that the church or its members are above the world or somehow live beyond the reality of sin. Here Melanchthon applied the theology of the cross to the church itself. Just as God's glory and salvation remain hidden in the lowly, shameful and even accursed cross of Christ (as in Gal 3:13), so the church exists in this life amid the mixed-up realities of law and gospel, death and life, sin and redemption. "For the kingdom of Christ is always that which he makes alive by his Spirit, whether it has been revealed or is hidden under the cross, just as Christ is the same, whether now glorified or previously afflicted."[19]

This ecclesiology of the cross means that the church will not be free of sin on this side of heaven, either among its individual members or as a wider community of faith. Instead, called into life by God, the church reflects the *simul iustus et peccator* (simultaneously justified and sinner) status of its people, whose lives continue to carry suffering and sin even as they live in the promises of baptism every day. One gathering at a time, the church needs to hear the truth about its sin, as well as the truth of God's mercy. More than being paralyzed by such conflicted realities, however, the Holy Spirit continues to create faith and set people free through the preaching of the gospel.

18. Ap 175.13.
19. Ap 176.18.

## Unity and Division in the Church

While the *Augsburg Confession* emphasized unity in the gospel, the *Apology* directly named conflict with the Church of Rome as a major obstacle to harmony and concord. Returning to the critiques of papal authority that Luther laid out in his 1520 *Address to the Christian Nobility of the German Nation*,[20] Melanchthon identified the issue:

> Perhaps the opponents demand that the church be defined as the supreme external monarchy of the entire world, in which the Roman pontiff must hold unlimited power, which no one is allowed to question or censure. This means the power to establish articles of faith and to cast aside the Scriptures as he wishes, to institute forms of worship and sacrifices, and likewise to frame whatever laws he wishes or to excuse and exempt people from any laws (divine, canonical, or civil), as he wishes. . . . Indeed, this is not a definition of the church of Christ but of the papal kingdom, according to the definition not only of the canonists but also of Daniel 11[:36-39].

> If we had defined the church in this way, we would probably have fairer judges. For there are in existence many extravagant and ungodly writings about the power of the Roman pontiff for which no one has ever been brought to trial. We alone are accused because we proclaim the blessings of Christ, namely, that we receive the forgiveness of sins by faith in Christ and not by religious rites invented by the pope. Moreover, Christ, the prophets, and the apostles define the church far differently than the papal kingdom.[21]

In his plea for the unity of the church, Melanchthon needed to name the papacy as the primary barrier to unity that the Lutheran reformers had encountered. Such language may not sound polite or diplomatic today, especially in light of the ecumenical interests shared in the Preface of this particular book. As we will discuss more in the next chapter, however, such direct statements belonged to the Lutheran conviction that God alone is the source of life and salvation, making it ever critical to name the things that get in the way of letting God be God. Also, Melanchthon and Luther had long been careful to note that

20. LW 44:126–39.
21. Ap 178.23-27.

their critique was not against structures or leaders in themselves but against institutions and leaders who put themselves in the place of God to give or judge righteousness.

Discussing the powerful role of the church's traditions in Reformation controversies, Melanchthon expressed disbelief that the Roman Church would insist so strongly upon relatively recent views of what is essential to salvation. Making use of a double negative to affirm the church's right to decide for itself what pleases God, the Roman Confutation had said "it is false that human ordinances instituted to placate God and make satisfaction for sin are against the Gospel."[22] In other words, the Confutation asserted that human rules about how to please God and atone for sin are consistent with the gospel.

To this Melanchthon replied, "Although we expected our opponents to defend human traditions for other reasons, we never dreamed that they would actually condemn the proposition that we do not merit the forgiveness of sins or grace by observing human traditions. Since they condemned this article, we have an open-and-shut case."[23] The Confutation had lifted up human ideas about salvation as being equally important to the teachings of scripture. Noting the difference between institutional conformity and spiritual unity, Melanchthon re-emphasized how much Lutherans respected and upheld much of the established Christian tradition. Rather than asserting Lutheran rights on this point, however, Melanchthon simply asked for Roman tolerance of evangelical reforms.

> Furthermore, we gladly keep the ancient traditions set up in the church because they are useful and promote tranquility, and we interpret them in the best possible way, by excluding the opinion that they justify. But our enemies falsely charge that we abolish good ordinances and church discipline. We can claim that the public liturgy is more dignified among us than among the opponents . . . Many among us celebrate the Lord's Supper every Lord's day after they are instructed, examined, and absolved. The children chant the Psalms in order to learn them; the people also sing in order either or to learn or to pray. Among our opponents there is no catechesis of children whatever, even though the canons prescribe it.

22. Kolb and Nestingen, 115.
23. Ap 223.3.

Among us, pastors and ministers of the church are required to instruct and examine the youth publicly, a custom that produces very good results.[24]

Throughout the *Apology*, Melanchthon grew increasingly passionate about the value of evangelical reforms and the harmful abuses that the reformers were working to correct. Rather than making absolute condemnations of the papacy, though, these critiques point repeatedly to the centrality of Jesus Christ as the righteousness of God for us. This righteousness does not come by pious works, by appeasing a few holy people, or even by belonging to the right institutional church; it comes purely by trusting the Lord alone to lead us into true life. People receive, live out, and share this faith through spiritual practices like regular participation in Holy Communion, singing Psalms and praying.

To show again that the Lutherans were not merely picking fights but genuinely desired Christian unity, Melanchthon admitted that the reformers would accept certain traditions and church regulations, as long as these did not obscure salvation through Christ alone.

Instead, in order to foster harmony [*concordia*], those ancient customs should be observed that can be observed without sin or without proving to be a great burden. In this very assembly we have sufficiently shown that, for the sake of love, we will reluctantly observe adiaphora with others, even if such things may prove to be somewhat burdensome. We judge that the greatest possible concord which can be maintained without offending consciences ought to be preferred to all other interests.[25]

For the sake of unity and concord, the Lutherans could observe practices and customs that they otherwise might have preferred to let go. Melanchthon called these "adiaphora," a Greek word meaning "undifferentiated": they are topics about which scripture does not give a firm rule. Such points of teaching and practice could be kept or dropped without harming unity and the saving message of the gospel. Early examples of adiaphora for the Lutherans included rules about

24. Ap 229.38-41.
25. Ap 230.52.

100

fasting or feasting, clerical vestments, and the practical organization of church life.

As Melanchthon put it near the end of the *Apology*, "We greatly wish for public harmony and peace, which is certainly fitting for Christians to cherish greatly among themselves."[26] Working against the cause of unity, the Church of Rome had rejected the central basis for Lutheran reforms—justification by faith—and was not willing to bend on other more practical points like the marriage of priests. Recognizing this institutional inflexibility, Melanchthon once again invoked Acts 5:29 and a true desire for harmony [*concordia*] in his final appeal to the emperor's wisdom and mercy.

Centuries later, these disputes over church practices, doctrine and unity can seem like obscure theological squabbles or cynical political maneuvers that have little to do with truly "spiritual" ideas about the church. This study has aimed to suggest something different. Faced with unyielding opposition from powerful adversaries, the Lutheran reformers described the one church of Christ in such a way that both they and their opponents could belong to it.

The early Lutherans were not Puritans, in the sense that the name Puritan refers to Protestant efforts "to purify the usage of the established church from the taint of popery."[27] On the contrary, despite serious conflicts with the Church of Rome, Lutherans sought tolerance, dialogue, and fellowship with Rome. If Rome still would not grant that, then the evangelicals would trust that they remained members of Christ's church on the basis of the preaching of the gospel and use of the sacraments.

In the *Apology*, Christian perfection never meant either the moral purity of individuals or the purified worship or organization of the church. As cited above, "On the contrary, perfection (that is, the integrity of the church) is preserved when the strong bear with the weak, when people put the best construction on the faults of their teachers, and when the bishops make some allowances for the

---

26. Ap 294.24-25.
27. A.G. Dickens, *The English Reformation*, 2nd ed. (University Park, PA: Pennsylvania State University Press, 1989), 368.

weakness of their people."[28] In this view, Christian perfection takes the shape of the cross. While sin remains in the individual lives and in the church's life together on this side of heaven, we find ourselves embraced by the total freedom and loving service that the cross brings.

## Repentance: Contrition and Faith

An important connection to make between the early Luther and the *Apology of the Augsburg Confession* arises in the *Apology*'s article on repentance, the theological issue behind the *95 Theses* that started the Reformation. While Melanchthon's discussion of repentance covers many technical points of penitential doctrines and practices, the following discussion focuses on the personal aspect of receiving the forgiveness of sins that the gospel promises. For the Lutherans, the reconciliation given in repentance offers "the very voice of the gospel itself, that we receive the forgiveness of sins by faith."[29]

In the medieval tradition, the sacrament of penance was described as having three parts: contrition (sorrow for sin), confession to a priest, and works of satisfaction. Already by 1519, though, Luther described the main parts of repentance as "contrition and faith"—that is, lamenting our sin and trusting God's word of forgiveness spoken by the pastor.[30] Consistent with this early teaching, the *Augsburg Confession* defined repentance as having the same two parts of contrition and faith.[31] Not surprisingly, the Roman Confutation rejected this evangelical view and re-affirmed the three part definition of penance.[32]

Another point of difference between the parties at Augsburg was that the Lutheran reformers asserted that believers could be certain of the forgiveness they received in repentance, because the God who promises forgiveness through the gospel is trustworthy. This "certainty of faith" stood in contrast to the dominant penitential theology of the time, which taught that confidence about being

28. Ap 155.234.
29. Ap 188.2.
30. LW 35:14.
31. CA XII 45.3–5.
32. Kolb and Nestingen, 113–14.

forgiven was a sin of pride. Additionally in the medieval tradition, believers might also continue to question the effectiveness of their confession: Were they truly sorry for their sins? Had they confessed all their sins correctly? Had they really done enough to make satisfaction for those sins or would they still be liable to punishment in hell or purgatory? Faced with these serious doubts, Lutheran reformers said that forgiveness does not depend on believers' penitential actions or attitudes but on the reliable word of God. God wants people to turn around—repent and believe in God—and promises forgiveness to all who hear and trust this word of reconciliation.

Focusing on the personal side of these issues, the Lutheran reformers focused on real experiences of sorrow and grace: "We say that contrition is the genuine terror of the conscience that feels God's wrath against sin and grieves that it has sinned;" then, "in the midst of these terrors, the gospel about Christ (which freely promises the forgiveness of sins through Christ) ought to be set forth to consciences" so that faith can hear and receive the promised word of release.[33] In this way, repentance is a personal experience of law and gospel rather than a ritual to perform or a state of spiritual purity to attain. As Melanchthon wrote, "We here understand repentance as the entire conversion, in which there are two sides, a putting to death and a raising to life."[34]

Connecting this repentance with the "faith mysticism" described earlier in this chapter, Melanchthon cited the medieval theologian Bernard of Clairvaux's description of the way believers move from despair to confidence because of faith in God's grace. According to Bernard, "Let everyone say in his anxiety: 'I will go to the gates of hell,' so that now we may take courage in no other way than in God's mercy alone. This is the trust of a person who forsakes self and relies on the Lord.'"[35] Faith in God's word provides spiritual deliverance and a blessedly restored connection with God in a way that one's own penitential efforts cannot achieve.

33. Ap 191.29, 192.35-36.
34. Ap 191.28.
35. Ap 196.58.

While the *Apology*'s words might have resonated with the spiritual worries of people in the sixteenth century, it is worth asking: do people in the early twenty-first century experience "genuine terror of the conscience" in any meaningful way or is this expression a relic of past modes of religious experience? Though the phrase "terror of the conscience" might sound foreign to many, people today certainly do experience profound troubles in body, mind and spirit. We regularly live with serious anxiety and legitimate fears about topics like personal worth, global climate change, social and domestic violence, discrimination, and economic inequality. While practical solutions abound, the spiritual side of these crises is rarely discussed: in the face of such massive social anxieties, people often suffer feelings of powerlessness and despair, anger and cynicism. The teaching about "contrition and faith," however, offers the chance to be honest about what sins and anxieties do to us. Instead of either ignoring or despairing of these immense problems around us, repentance invites us to trust the promises of scripture: "Surely there is a future, and your hope will not be cut off" (Prov 23:18); and, "The time is fulfilled, and the kingdom of God has come near; repent, and believe in the good news" (Mark 1:15).

Though today's worldviews may be significantly different from those of the Reformation, contrition and faith remain powerful resources for addressing the hard realities in which we often live, calling us to trust in God for life and to pray and serve the beloved creation around us. In a time like ours in which doomsayers and cynics easily overlook the power of simple acts of faith, hope, and love, the *Apology* offers the assurance that "faith is the new sentence that overturns the prior one and brings peace and life to the heart."[36] Contrition and faith send people back to the savior and Lord who continuously sustains life not because we have earned it but because God loves this world so much. In repentance and faith, we get to be part of that love.

36. Ap 195.48.

## Conclusion: Melanchthon's Confession

Near the end of the *Apology*, Melanchthon gave a personal testimony to the power of faith to change the world, to help endure hardships and to live into the promised forgiveness, freedom, and life of God. Recognizing the powerful obstacles that he and other Reformation-minded people faced, he made a personal confession of his faith in God.

> Now when our consciences realize that our opponents condemn the manifest truth—the defense of which is necessary for the church and extols the glory of Christ—we can easily despise the terrors of the world and patiently bear whatever we have to suffer on account of the glory of Christ and the welfare of the church. Who would not gladly die in the confession of these articles: that by faith we receive the forgiveness of sins freely on account of Christ and that we do not merit the forgiveness of sins by our works? The consciences of the godly will not have sufficiently firm consolation against the terrors of sin and death or against the devil's inciting them to despair, unless they know that they ought to stand firmly upon the fact that they have the forgiveness of sins freely on account of Christ. This faith sustains and enlivens hearts in their most bitter struggles with despair.[37]

The *Apology of the Augsburg Confession* shows Melanchthon and the evangelicals ready to stand firm in their faith in God, despite the threats of the powers-that-be and despite the despair and doubts of their own hearts. This conviction served as a source of strength and compassion, based upon faith in a God who transforms hearts, minds and hands, individuals, and communities.

37. Ap 236.6-8.

6

———

# Freedom and Service in the
# *Smalcald Articles*

Luther's *Smalcald Articles* stand as something of an enigma in the Book of Concord. Given all of Luther's important works, why does this later document receive such a privileged place in the Confessions of the Evangelical Lutheran Church? Further, because these articles contain Luther's sharp language against all manner of opponents, they can be viewed as "too Lutheran," reflecting an unhelpful partisanship supposedly typical of the later Luther and rigid Lutheran Orthodoxy.[1]

In the face of such questions, this chapter interprets the *Smalcald Articles* as a positive statement for Christian freedom, which presents a theological and ecclesiastical legacy from the late Luther that resonates with his stirring words of liberation from the early Reformation. In this work, faith in Christ alone stands at the center of the church's witness, bringing the blessed effects of both radical freedom and radical service.

---

1. William R. Russell, *Luther's Theological Testament: The Schmalkald Articles* (Minneapolis: Fortress, 1995), 14.

## Luther's Last Theological Will and Testament

Reformation historian William Russell has made the convincing case that the *Smalcald Articles* represent Luther's "last theological will and testament," which has a twofold meaning, one political and one personal.[2] From the political side, Luther wrote these articles beginning in December 1536 at the request of his sovereign prince, Elector John Frederick of Saxony. Pope Paul III had called for a church council, and, though it would not meet until 1545 at Trent, the Lutherans needed to decide how to prepare for such a gathering of the church. In February 1537, the evangelical lands that had banded together for mutual self-defense (the Smalcald League) met in the town of Smalcald. There the theologians discussed and signed Luther's articles as a statement of their shared faith. Although the politicians eventually decided to re-affirm the *Augsburg Confession* as the primary expression of evangelical faith, Luther published the *Smalcald Articles* in 1538 as a way to reaffirm his theology and highlight agreement with his colleagues two decades after the start of the Reformation.

Adding personal urgency, Luther was deathly ill in late 1536 and early 1537.[3] Discussions with Wittenberg colleagues on these articles in December 1536, for instance, were interrupted when Luther suffered a heart attack. Then, after feeling well enough to travel to Smalcald the following February, Luther could not participate in the dialogue because of kidney stones. These prevented him from urinating for several days and nearly proved fatal. Luther left the conference early in an effort to die closer to home. The bumpy carriage ride, however, seems to have loosened the blockage and led to his recovery.

While the "last theological will and testament" nature of the articles could possibly lend the *Smalcald Articles* a grave or severe tone, the document itself conveys a confident, conversational air. This might be surprising unless we consider its author's personal and professional

---

2. For more on the background of the *Smalcald Articles*, see Russell, *Luther's Theological Testament*, and William R. Russell, "The Smalcald Articles: Luther's Theological Testament," in *Lutheran Quarterly* 5 (Autumn 1991), 277–96. See also, Arand, Kolb, and Nestingen, 139–60.

3. Russell, 24–33; and Martin Brecht, *Martin Luther: The Preservation of the Church, 1532-1546*, translated by James Schaaf (Minneapolis: Fortress, 1993), 173–88.

familiarity with matters of life and death. Consistent with so many of his other works—including his *Sermon on Preparing to Die* (1519)[4] and the *Confession Concerning Christ's Supper* (1528)[5]—the *Smalcald Articles* emphasize the comforting and empowering freedom from sin, death and the devil that comes through the gospel, blessings to which Luther could testify firsthand.

## Gospel Freedom and Gospel Service

At this point in his career, Luther refused to add new rules or definitions for believers to follow. The evangelical church that would continue after his death should be a church rooted in the gospel alone, free to preach, worship, and serve in whatever flexible, contextual ways would best serve preaching, ministry, and mission. "God be praised," he wrote, "a seven-year-old-child knows what the church is: holy believers and 'the little sheep who hear the voice of their shepherd.'"[6] Instead of writing more about what people and churches ought to do, Luther emphasized the blessings of God by keeping his message simple.

Luther's preface to these articles made clear that this simplicity was intentional and not a way to dodge careful attention to doctrinal or organizational detail. Wanting to avoid long debates about contested points of theology and Christian life, Luther wrote:

> I, therefore, have provided only a few articles, because in any case we already have received from God so many mandates to carry out in the church, in the government, and in the home that we can never fulfill them. What is the point, what is the use of making so many decretals and regulations in the council, especially if no one honors or observes the chief things commanded by God? It is as if God had to honor our buffoonery while in return we trample his solemn commands under foot.[7]

Christians do not need to add new things to God's word and to church life. This focus on simplicity resonates with something Luther wrote

4. LW 42:99–115.
5. LW 37:360–72.
6. SA 324.2.
7. SA 300.14.

in the *Large Catechism*: the Ten Commandments alone give Christians enough to do for a lifetime.[8] Further, the citation above shows Luther highlighting the importance of serving God and neighbor within the three estates God created for people to live in: church, government, and home (which for Luther also meant economic life).

Gospel-centered simplicity also leaves Christians free to stop fighting over words and start to do the concrete work that the world so desperately needs, those "countless important matters in worldly affairs" that—as he described it—included overcoming political divisions, economic injustice, and "conspicuous consumption" among all classes.[9] For Luther, engaging these practical issues of daily life was more important than revisiting overworked and unfruitful theological ground. Either Christians live in the faith that they have received through word and sacrament, or they are busying themselves with unnecessary things and forgetting to live out the faith in the places and ways God has already given.

As in *The Freedom of a Christian* (1520) and articles 6 and 20 of the *Augsburg Confession*, Luther wrote that good works come from justifying faith; they are always effects of faith, never causes. In the *Smalcald Articles*, this emphasis appears in a section entitled "How a Person is Justified and Concerning Good Works." The later Luther remained as dedicated to effective social action as he ever had been, consistently making the case that social reform is a godly fruit of faith in God's mercy. He wrote,

> I cannot change at all what I have consistently taught about this until now, namely, that "though faith" (as St. Peter says [Acts 15:9]) we receive a different, new, clean heart and that , for the sake of Christ our mediator, God will and does regard us as completely righteous and holy. Although sin in the flesh is still not completely gone or dead, God will nevertheless not count it or consider it.

> Good works follow such faith, renewal, and forgiveness of sin, and whatever in these works is still sinful or imperfect should not even be counted as sin or imperfection, precisely for the sake of this same

8. SA 382.16.
9. SA 299.12.

Christ. . . . Therefore we cannot boast about the great merit of our works, where they are viewed apart from grace and mercy. Rather, as it is written, "Let the one who boasts, boast in the Lord [1 Cor 1:31; 2 Cor 10:17]." That is, if one has a gracious God, then everything is good. Furthermore, we also say that if good works do not follow, then faith is false and not true.[10]

In terms of Christian mission and service, this meant that Luther cared about good preaching not only for its internal spiritual value but also because of the important good works done for others that come from the Holy Spirit's activity in the lives of people who trust God above all else.

From this conviction, the *Smalcald Articles* present a clear Evangelical Lutheran view of the church's mission: faith in God frees people from internal fears and external demands, leaving them with nothing to do but serve others selflessly. Within the church, there is tremendous room for freedom, flexibility, conservation, or reform in structures and practices, just so long as the gospel is being announced and received. With this message, the *Smalcald Articles* stand as a worthy theological bookend to the groundbreaking works of Luther's early career.

## Luther's Method

Luther's commitment to keeping the gospel central and expressing it simply also helps us better understand his theology and method. His theological education had been influenced by the "nominalist" branch of medieval scholasticism founded by the English Franciscan William of Occam (ca. 1287–1347). Occam's influence still appears today in the phrase "Occam's razor," which means that simpler, more direct explanations are preferred to more complicated ones. Though he broke from other aspects of nominalism, Luther appreciated the clarity and precision of Occam's thought, which had allowed Occam to cut to the heart of theological issues and to "guard against false conclusions."[11]

Luther's entire career, including the *Smalcald Articles*, shows a keen

---

10. SA 325.1-3.
11. Brecht, *Martin Luther: His Road to Reformation 1483-1521*, 37.

ability to get to the heart of things. Faced with the likelihood that a Roman council would once again reject evangelical reforms and perspectives in the mid-1530s, Luther made the issues as straightforward as possible. Having discussed justification and reforms of the Mass, monasticism, and papal authority, Luther concluded his opening section by writing, "These four articles will furnish them with enough to condemn at the council. They neither can nor will concede to us the tiniest fraction of these articles."[12]

Such a summary may sound cynical or harsh. If so, we might recall that the Council of Trent did, in fact, reject the evangelical views of these topics without an open discussion of them.[13] Rather than waste time and energy dancing around the issues, Luther recognized that evangelical churches would be better served by simply confessing and living out their gospel faith as clearly as possible. The *Smalcald Articles* provide a good example of how Luther preferred to simplify and clarify rather than add new teachings. In this method, Luther left a useful legacy of directness that continues to be worth claiming.

### The First and Chief Article

In the *Smalcald Articles*, Luther returned to his longstanding conviction that the papal church needed to be resisted insofar as it had added conditions to salvation and obscured Christ alone as the one who reconciles people with God and each other through extra works and rituals. Addressing the more radical side of the Reformation, he also rejected "enthusiasts" who wanted to find salvation and spirituality apart from the scriptures and the church's means of grace. At one point, he even identified the papacy and radical reformers as guilty of the same basic error: in his view, both groups defined salvation in terms of their own ideas about holiness, with the papacy insisting on its rules and radical reformers insisting on a higher spirituality than the New Testament presented.[14]

---

12. SA 310.15.
13. Justification by faith alone, for instance, was rejected in the Council of Trent's sixth session (1547); other points were addressed in later sessions; *Enchiridion Symbolorum*, 33rd ed., Heinrich Denzinger and Adolf Schönmetzer, eds. (Rome: Herder, 1965), 378–79.

More than simply attacking those who disagreed with him, Luther lifted up the preaching of the gospel as the only reliable source of faith and life, making who Christ is and what he does the "first and chief article" of evangelical teaching. Since "God alone is righteous and justifies the one who has faith in Jesus," believers cannot make themselves righteous but receive God's external righteousness passively by trusting themselves to God; that is, through faith alone.[15] "On this article," Luther wrote, "stands all that we teach and practice against the pope, the devil, and the world. Therefore we must be quite certain and have no doubt about it."[16] In Luther's reading of the Bible, justification by faith alone is the essential point to hold on to because of how it simultaneously frees people from all other powers and is the only thing that leads to truly selfless works of love.

From this conviction, Luther insisted on the Christian freedom he had been teaching since his early career. Reconciled to God through faith alone in Christ alone, Christians are free from any other work or requirement for salvation. Grounded in such freedom, church practices ought to be reformed accordingly, with the doctrine of justification serving as a kind of Occam's razor. Luther discussed practices to keep, reform, tolerate or reject on the basis of how they helped or hindered the gospel message of God's free justification of the ungodly. Along those lines, the *Smalcald Articles* considered subjects like the right use of the Mass, purgatory, pilgrimages, relics, indulgences, and the invocation of the saints.[17] Insofar as any of these practices or concepts would aid or obscure salvation by faith, a gospel-centered church would have the freedom to reject or reform them.

Luther's own life story entered the *Smalcald Articles* when he started to describe the meaning of repentance. Recalling all the works he had done in the monastery to gain forgiveness, he repeatedly observed that in those days "no one knew" how much contrition was needed, whether they had confessed adequately, whether they had sufficiently

---

14. SA 322.3-6.
15. SA 300–301.4, citing Rom 3:26, 28.
16. SA 301.5.
17. These topics are the subject of SA 301–6.

completed their penitential works of satisfaction, or which souls needed more or less relief in purgatory. Contrasting those uncertainties with the gospel call to repent and believe, Luther wrote that this had meant that he was "always doing penance but never arriving at repentance."[18]

Reading the *Smalcald Articles* as a call to preserve the church's freedom and point to liberating repentance and faith allows readers today to see that this document does not merely attack Luther's sixteenth-century adversaries, whether radical groups or the papacy. On the contrary, these articles call for all Christians to trust their hearts and their churches to Christ alone. Rules and regulations—even well-intentioned religious ones—cannot give life or reconciliation. If such rules or practices serve the gospel , then they are worth keeping. When human ideas about holiness obscure the gospel, however, they need to be set aside. One can tell whether any such regulation is good, bad or indifferent based on its relationship to the chief article of justification by faith alone in Christ alone.

Instead of promoting the view that his side was completely right and everyone else was wrong, Luther taught that faith is a lifelong journey of repentance under the cross. In language similar to the *95 Theses* and the *Small Catechism*, he wrote:

> This repentance endures among Christians until death because it struggles with the sin that remains in the flesh throughout life. As St. Paul bears witness in Romans 7[:23], he wars with the law in his members, etc. – not by using his own powers but with the gift of the Holy Spirit which follows from the forgiveness of sins. This same gift daily cleanses and sweeps away the sins that remain and works to make people truly pure and holy.[19]

As we saw in Melanchthon's *Apology of the Augsburg Confession*, Christian perfection is not a work of the Christian but the ongoing work of the Holy Spirit to lead people into forgiveness through the cross. Reminscent of the *Heidelberg Disputation*, Luther continued to value

18. SA 315.23. Further autobiographical reflection appears at 316.28.
19. SA 318.40.

"calling a thing what it is" and being honest about human sin (including pride and self-centeredness) and clinging to the incredible truth of divine mercy. More than just a theological program or a narrow set of ideological commitments, the *Smalcald Articles* express the principles Luther believed were most important for keeping gospel freedom at the center of the Christian life.

## Luther and Melanchthon

Part of the story about the *Smalcald Articles* sometimes includes mention of a growing rift between Luther and Melanchthon, particularly on the issues of Holy Communion and continuing dialogue with other Christians. In preparing for a potential council, for instance, the two reformers held some different perspectives: Luther was more open to the older practice of ordination by bishops than Melanchthon; Melanchthon was more willing to see the Church of Rome allow communion in both kinds for the evangelicals without reforming that practice for whole church, as Luther wanted.[20] Regarding core commitments, however, Luther and Melanchthon remained quite close.

On Holy Communion, for instance, the *Smalcald Articles* state: "We maintain that the bread and the wine in the Supper are the true body and blood of Christ and that they are not only offered to and received by upright Christians but also by evil ones."[21] According to some, this direct formulation conflicts with the *Wittenberg Concord*, which Lutherans—including Luther—had signed with south German reformers like Martin Bucer and Wolfgang Capito in 1536, and which says that Christ is present "under the bread and the wine."[22] Because Melanchthon had composed the articles of the *Wittenberg Concord*, Luther's words at Smalcald might then indicate his dissatisfaction with Melanchthon and the *Wittenberg Concord* that he had previously approved.

---

20. Brecht, *Martin Luther: The Preservation of the Church, 1532-1546*, 181.
21. SA 320.1.
22. SA 320, footnote 136.

Evidence for this potential conflict appears in a report from the meeting at Smalcald in which the influential reforming prince Philip of Hesse reported Melanchthon's disappointment that the *Smalcald Articles* did not match the *Wittenberg Concord* more exactly.[23] While these words may describe Melanchthon's view accurately, it should be noted that the *Smalcald Articles'* words about communion differ not only from the *Wittenberg Concord* but also from the *Small Catechism, Large Catechism,* and *Augsburg Confession,* which each say that Christ is present "in" or "under" the bread and wine.[24] Lutherans emphasized these prepositions in order to affirm the real presence of Christ in the sacrament without accepting the Roman teaching of transubstantiation, in which the substance of the communion elements ceases to be bread and wine and instead becomes the body and blood of Christ.

Luther's expression in the *Smalcald Articles* certainly matches the longstanding Lutheran understanding of Christ's real presence in communion based on a straightforward interpretation of the words "this is my body . . . this is my blood" from Matt 26:26-28. Nevertheless, because Radical, Reformed, Lutheran, and Roman Catholic Christians of the period all interpreted the words "this is my body" differently, Luther's use of Matthew 26 might not have been as helpful here as he supposed. In that light, Melanchthon's objection would not mean that he disagreed with Luther's view of the Lord's Supper but with the potential for misunderstanding that came by simply citing Matthew 26 without further comment.

The issue of papal supremacy represents another point on which Luther and Melanchthon expressed themselves differently. In the *Smalcald Articles,* Luther wrote,

> the pope is not the head of all Christendom "by divine right" or on the basis of God's Word, because that belongs only to the one who is called Jesus Christ. Instead, the pope is only bishop, or pastor, of the church at Rome and of those who willingly or through a human institution (that

23. Cited in Hans Volz, ed., *Urkunden und Aketenstücke zur Geschichte von Martin Luthers Schmalkaldischen Artikeln (1536-1574)* (Berlin: de Gruyter, 1957), 104–5.
24. CA X 44.1, SC 362.1-2, and LC 467.8.

116

is, through secular authority) have joined themselves to him in order to be Christians alongside him as a brother and companion but not under him as a lord—as the ancient councils and the time of St. Cyprian demonstrate.[25]

Here Luther returned to his early conflicts with Rome and expressed the same view that can be found, among other places, in the letter to Pope Leo X that introduces *The Freedom of a Christian*.[26] Luther acknowledged—and was willing to honor—the papacy as a human institution but not as a divinely-given authority over all Christians. Though Luther granted the possibility in the *Smalcald Articles* that a supreme head of the church might govern "by human right" with the consent of the people, he did not believe that such a thing would happen for two reasons: people would not elect such a universal leader and the papacy itself would not approve of power based on mere human authority.[27]

For his part, Melanchthon signed the *Smalcald Articles* with the proviso that he might accept papal rule "by human right" if the papacy would allow the evangelical preaching of the gospel.

> I, Philip Melanthon, also regard the above articles as true and Christian. However, concerning the pope I maintain that if he would allow the gospel, we, too, may (for the sake of peace and general unity among those Christians who are now under him and might be in the future) grant to him his superiority over the bishops which he has "by human right."[28]

Far from differing with Luther's view of the papacy, Melanchthon affirmed it, while leaving the door for dialogue with Rome slightly more open. First, he agreed with Luther in saying that there is no scriptural sanction for the pope to rule "by divine right." Second, he agreed that it would be legitimate to live under papal authority with the understanding that such a form of church government was a matter of freedom that does not concern salvation. Third, his statement accentuated that the burden of unity would fall on the papal

---

25. SA 307.1.
26. Luther, *The Freedom of a Christian*, 35–38.
27. SA 308.7.
28. SA 326, and footnote 172: "Melanchthon began spelling his name 'Melanthon' in 1521."

church to "allow the gospel," not on the Lutherans to accept papal authority. Though they framed their views differently, Luther and Melanchthon agreed about these central issues of faith, unity, and church order.

The fact that Luther and Melanchthon had different ways of expressing themselves is not a liability but a gift of the Reformation, exemplifying the Christian freedom and flexibility that Lutheran theology teaches. Through the gospel, people are free to be themselves and do not need to be clones of Luther, Melanchthon, or anyone else. If a difference between Luther and Melanchthon arose in the *Smalcald Articles*, then it is one that highlights rather than undermines Luther's teaching of Christian freedom and the unity that comes through faith.

## Treatise on the Power and Primacy of the Pope

We can see Luther and Melanchthon's fundamental agreement on the gospel and church authority in the *Treatise on the Power and Primacy of the Pope.* In fact, their views were so close that by 1580 Lutherans believed that Luther himself had written the *Treatise*.[29]

At the 1537 meeting in Smalcald, Lutheran political leaders decided to stand upon the *Augsburg Confession* and its *Apology* as their statement of faith at a future council. Since the *Augsburg Confession* had not included an article on the papacy, Melanchthon was asked to write such a supplement. The *Treatise* can therefore be read as a kind of "article 29" added to the original 28 articles of the *Augustana*. In his typical well-organized manner, Melanchthon began the *Treatise* by immediately identifying three main points of dissent.

> The bishop of Rome [the pope] claims to be superior by divine right to all bishops and pastors. In addition, he claims to possess by divine right the power of both swords, that is, the authority to confer and transfer royal [secular] authority. Third, he states that it is necessary for salvation to believe these things. For these reasons the Roman bishop calls himself the vicar of Christ on earth. We hold and publicly declare that these three articles of faith are false, impious, tyrannical, and ruinous to the church.[30]

29. BC 330 (editor's introduction).
30. Tr 330.1-4.

Having identified the primary issues, Melanchthon provided Lutheran objections to the papacy of the day on the basis of the Bible, early church writers, and other examples from history. His three points recollected the "three walls" that Luther described in his 1520 tract *To the Christian Nobility of the German Nation.* In that tract, Luther asserted that the papacy protected its power by unjustly claiming authority over all other rulers, over all church councils, and over the interpretation of the Bible.[31]

The Lutherans did not object to institutions, hierarchy, or authority in general. Instead, they opposed the specific claim that God had established "by divine right" a single head over Christendom besides Jesus Christ. As Luther pointed out in the *Smalcald Articles,* the evangelicals would be willing to accept a single head of the church "by human right" as a sign of Christian unity and practical aid for organization. But the strong resistance that the Lutherans encountered when they described the papacy as anything less than divine made them pessimistic about that possibility. This insistence that the pope only ruled "by human right" gave Melanchthon's note in his endorsement of the *Smalcald Articles* its edge. The Lutherans would accept institutional unity with Rome only if it meant a thorough reform of the papacy.

Melanchthon's second point against papal supremacy over secular governments repeated one that Luther had long held. This matter of the "two swords" (the authority of church and state) had been controversial in medieval Christendom, especially during the Investiture Controversy of the eleventh and twelfth centuries; the papacy had mostly won that debate, gaining authority for popes and bishops to install secular leaders, instead of the other way around.[32] In contrast to this view, Lutherans taught that political governments were themselves God-given tools for serving the common good and, as such, could be free from direct church oversight in matters of civil governance. While governments exist for the sake of serving daily life,

---

31. LW 44:126–37.
32. On the Investiture Controversy, see Justo González, *The Story of Christianity, Volume 1: The Early Church to the Reformation,* Revised and Updated (New York: HarperCollins, 2010), 338–44.

the church's primary mission is the different task of delivering God's means of grace. For the Lutherans, the church wields its authority (the "sword") correctly when it announces law and gospel to individuals and communities, not by building up power to rule secular affairs.

Even hypothetically granting papal supremacy over church and state, however, Melanchthon believed that mere submission to any pope or papal rule would never reconcile people to God or each other. He wrote, "Even if the Roman bishop possessed primacy and superiority by divine right, one would still not owe obedience to those pontiffs who defend ungodly forms of worship, idolatry, and teaching inimical to the gospel."[33] Melanchthon then cited Bible verses about resisting false teachings (including Acts 5:29) and even quoted papal laws which "clearly teach that a heretical pope is not to be obeyed."[34]

Lutherans today do not need to view these strong sixteenth-century statements against the papacy as once-and-for-all condemnations of Roman Catholicism or its leaders. Instead, Timothy Wengert has suggested that these words apply to "all kinds of self-appointed keepers of the public good and morals." In both the *Smalcald Articles* and the *Treatise*, Lutheran critiques were not aimed at popes or Roman Catholicism as such. Instead, the reformers confronted the constant temptation to turn human ideas and structures into gods. Wengert's observation continues with examples of sinful power struggles in the present:

> When pastors keep their congregants' consciences bound to the pastors' own moral opinions; when congregations demand that pastors and bishops be little more than hired hands and censure them for pointing out the political ramifications of Christian faith; when pastors, bishops, or entire churches claim to be anything more than faithful Christians fulfilling their vocations in the world: then the same kind of tyranny and confusion of faith and Christ's reign with political success threaten the church.[35]

33. Tr 336.38.
34. Tr 336.38.
35. Timothy Wengert, *Priesthood, Pastors, Bishops: Public Ministry for the Reformation and Today* (Minneapolis: Fortress, 2008), 91.

Luther and Melanchthon's critiques of the papacy speak against all misuse of power in the church, abuses which break the first commandment by making human ideas about salvation into gods, judges, and saviors. Instead, the gospel lets God be God and encourages lives of mutual respect and servant leadership.

Connecting theological arguments about church leadership with pastoral care, Melanchthon's *Treatise* expressed two points of practical concern that had arisen in the conflicts with Rome. First, the Roman view of authority had led to violence against persons and lands over time, including the martyrdom of early Protestants.[36] Second, the papacy had prevented the holding of free and open councils that might have served the church's health, unity, and mutual accountability. "Thus the pope exercises a double tyranny: he defends his errors with violence and murder, and he forbids judicial inquiry."[37]

Faced with accusations that the Lutheran reformers had divided Christendom and spread discord through their work and teachings, Melanchthon wrote, "all the godly have good, compelling, and clear reasons not to submit to the pope. These reasons console them in the face of all the reproaches for causing scandal, schism, and discord, with which they are regularly taunted."[38] Luther and Melanchthon did not reject institutions or even institutional power structures. Instead, they advocated for institutions that are aware of their own capacity for sin and practice basic care for bodies and souls.

## Conclusion: Lutherans and Church Structure

As a movement that came into being through resistance, Lutheranism has frequently struggled with the meaning of "church authority." The historical context of resisting a hierarchy built an anti-authoritarian or anti-institutional element into Lutheran church life. A temptation can then arise to equate anti-institutional ideas with faithfulness to the gospel. However, the Lutheran reformers never viewed resistance itself

---

36. Tr 337.40 and footnote 44.
37. Tr 338–339.49-51.
38. Tr 339.58.

as the main point of their efforts. On the contrary, they very much lamented the need to resist and only invoked verses like Acts 5:29 out of specific cases of urgency.

While this Lutheran ambivalence about institutions and authority can certainly become a liability, it also reveals a strength. The word "dialectic" again comes into play. Between the extremes of either worshiping or disparaging earthly institutions, the reformers hoped their people would reflect daily on how best to respond in meaningful, socially responsible ways to the inevitable needs of a fallen world. They built this attitude on the belief that church, government, and families—the three estates—were God-given blessings for life together, even with their imperfections.

Lutherans also taught that because all Christians share the equal spiritual status given in baptism, there should be no spiritual hierarchy on the basis of monastic vows or institutional honors. All the baptized share an equal spiritual status before God and each other. At the same time, this spiritual equality did not remove the Lutherans' concern for different orders of ministry, including pastoral ministry and the office of oversight, that is, bishops. Beginning in the 1530s Lutherans installed superintendents to do the work of bishops, responsible for overseeing good teaching, ministry, and concord in particular areas. As Melanchthon wrote in the closing to the *Treatise*, "The gospel bestows upon those who preside over the churches [pastors and bishops] the commission to proclaim the gospel, forgive sins, and administer the sacraments."[39] As discussed in article 5 of the *Augsburg Confession*, God does not leave the church without stewards to oversee preaching, teaching, worship, and community life, but the Holy Spirit creates the office of ministry as a means of sharing the gospel. These ministers are not lords over other Christians but rather are sent out to make sure the gospel is being shared and experienced. In that way, preaching the gospel is the task of ordained ministry just like teaching math is the job of a math teacher; overseeing church ministries more broadly is the task of a bishop, just like principals oversee the different aspects

39. Tr 340.60.

of a school. Whether Christians are in positions of either authority or service, working inside or outside the church, the words of Luke 17 remind all alike to say about their work, "we have only done what we ought to have done."

Rather than upholding either an authoritarian or anti-institutional model, Lutherans of the Reformation era aimed to avoid extreme positions, focusing instead on being faithful to Christ in whatever ways the context demanded. The church's freedom and flexibility to organize itself to best serve the gospel is an intentional legacy and strength passed on through the Lutheran Confessions, especially in Luther's *Smalcald Articles* and Melanchthon's *Treatise on the Power and Primacy of the Pope*.

7

---

# A Model for Harmony:
# the *Formula of Concord*

The 1577 *Formula of Concord* provides an important test case for this study. Did later Lutherans lose the practical and spiritual concerns that drove Luther and Melanchthon's works? Did the passionate faith of the early Reformation turn into a set of rigid, impersonal and unspiritual dogmas? Was harmony a serious value or did the word *concordia* become a cynical cover for power-hungry leaders? This chapter aims to show that sincere interest in mutual dialogue, intellectual honesty and communal well-being survived beyond the early Lutheran Reformation and are visible in the *Formula of Concord*.

While we recall that concord means harmony, we can also experience this document in new ways by reconsidering the word Formula. In Latin, "formula" not only means a strict rule like we use in mathematics but it can mean something like a charter, model or paradigm. As a "model for harmony," therefore, the *Formula of Concord* gives an example of how later Lutherans expressed their shared understandings of faith and life together in ways that made sense for their time, leaving an important witness for those who would come after them.

The fact that the *Formula of Concord* held legal status as the official expression of Christian faith in lands that accepted it adds a complicating factor to its legacy. We rightly ask hard questions about the potentially corrupting relationships between political power and religious formulations; historians have made many fascinating studies of these issues.[1] Because I suspect that modern political groups will probably not choose the *Formula of Concord* as a preferred tool of social coercion anytime soon, I would like to lay such questions aside for now. Instead, following the pattern of our earlier chapters, I suggest that we will get to know the *Formula of Concord* more profitably as a spiritual resource for individual and communal use.

## Lutherans after Luther

To understand the 1577 *Formula of Concord* as a model for harmony, we need to examine some of its historical context. As Lutheranism spread in the 1530s and 1540s, each city or territory that embraced these reforms adopted a new evangelical church order that explained how it would organize its religious teaching, worship and institutional life. Between the years 1523 and 1555, "no fewer than 135 church orders appeared" in Lutheran lands, a sign of the geographical diversity—not theological divisions—of early Lutherans.[2] Luther Reed, a twentieth-century scholar of Lutheran worship, described the early Reformation church orders in this way:

> Though differing greatly in minor details, they were pervaded by an inner unity of purpose and plan. This was due to the far-reaching influence of Luther and also to the fact that the most important of the orders were prepared by theologians who had a common understanding as to general principles of procedure. Since most of the Reformers helped to prepare several orders each (Bugenhagen seven, [Johannes] Brenz five, [Justus]

1. For instance, the collection of essays in Robert Kolb, ed., *Lutheran Ecclesiastical Culture, 1550-1675* (Leiden: Brill, 2008).
2. Luther D. Reed, *The Lutheran Liturgy* (Philadelphia: Muhlenberg, 1947), 89.

Jonas four, etc.), it is possible to group the orders in families and trace the influence which the most important ones exerted upon others.[3]

These local Lutheran church orders embodied the *Augsburg Confession*'s principle that unity in gospel teaching allowed for diversity in local practice. As Reed noted, different territories could express their faith and organize their churches in ways that made sense for their contexts, while also remaining more broadly connected to other Lutheran communities.

New challenges arose in the later 1540s, especially after Martin Luther's death on February 18, 1546. Although Luther had always worked closely with his colleagues, he personified and symbolized the Reformation movement that bore his name like no other. Having died away from home while mediating a political dispute in his birthplace of Eisleben, Luther's body was taken back to Wittenberg and buried in the Castle Church. Bugenhagen preached the funeral sermon on St. Paul's words in 1 Thess 4:13-14: "But we do not want you to be uninformed, brothers and sisters, about those who have died, so that you may not grieve as others do who have no hope. For since we believe that Jesus died and rose again, even so, through Jesus, God will bring with him those who have died."[4] Expressing the grief of a community that had just lost its leader, Bugenhagen's sermon also preached the hope and comfort of God's eternal gospel, which Luther had dedicated his life to learning and sharing.

Philip Melanchthon delivered the eulogy for Luther. In the words of Luther biographer Martin Brecht, Melanchthon told the grieving assembly that "It was not human intelligence from which the doctrine of the forgiveness of sins and trust in the Son of God had come, but God who had revealed it to Luther."[5] Thus, Melanchthon immediately interpreted Luther's central teaching in terms of the free forgiveness given to sinners through faith in Jesus Christ. Melanchthon also

---

3. Reed, 89.
4. Bugenhagen, "A Christian Sermon over the Body and at the Funeral of the Venerable Dr. Martin Luther" in *Bugenhagen, Selected Writings, Volume 1*, 111–23. Also available online: http://beck.library.emory.edu/luther/luther_site/luther_text.html.
5. Brecht, *Martin Luther: The Preservation of the Church*, 1532-1546, 378–79.

encouraged the people to honor Luther's life and work because his death appeared to be an evil omen of things to come.[6] While this may sound unnecessarily dramatic, Melanchthon's sense that hard times were coming proved quite true.

Before we discuss the years that followed, however, something else that Brecht observed about Melanchthon's eulogy stands out: Melanchthon already started the work of understanding Luther's complex legacy as a person and as a leader. As Brecht's own monumental biography of Luther came to a close, he wrote:

> In his eulogy Melanchthon was the first to give an extensive evaluation of Luther's life after his death. Despite certain reservations, he wanted to make a positive statement. The address has therefore become a notable document because it did not simply employ the obvious reasons for praising Luther. As a man, Luther was also a problem for his closest theological co-worker, and he had repeatedly suffered under him until the end. Melanchthon was so honest that he could not refrain from mentioning this, but he tried instead to give a sympathetic explanation. Anyone who thoroughly explores the peaks and valleys of Luther's long and complex life confronts the same problem. Wherever we place him, we are also free to criticize him; this detracts not at all from his greatness. Like every biographer, Melanchthon evaluated Luther from his own personal and theological standpoint, and he chose to accent certain things accordingly. Thus he lifted up the significance of pure doctrine, with justification by faith as its center, as the heritage that was scrupulously to be preserved. This inaugurated the new age of "Lutheranism." ... His own political and ecclesiastical interests did not prevent Melanchthon from also perceiving the political and social significance of Luther's thought or certain features of his piety and human qualities. For Melanchthon, Luther's historical dimension and his calling consisted in his action—in the succession of the great teachers of the people of God—of again bringing evangelical truth to light, which inexorably led to a great conflict. In total agreement with Luther, this was for him an event that took place not only within this world. Luther's first biographer had already accurately perceived his person and work (both theologically and historically) as more than something that affected the history of the world—as a continuing challenge.[7]

From February 1546 onward, Lutherans after Luther inherited a legacy

---

6. Ibid.
7. Brecht, *Martin Luther: The Preservation of the Church, 1532-1546*, 381–82.

in which truth is not just something to recite, but something to live, experience, struggle with, and share in meaningful ways. How would the next generation of Lutherans relate their quests for spiritual faithfulness to the hard questions of their time? The *Formula of Concord* represents that second generation's attempts to care for body and soul in faithful and flexible ways.

## A Generation of Conflict

Melanchthon's assertion that Lutherans in Germany were soon to encounter hard times proved accurate. Around the same time as Luther's death, Emperor Charles had finally secured peace on his borders and was making plans to restore religious unity in his lands by force. The Smalcaldic War between Emperor Charles and Lutheran states began in the second half of 1546. In the following spring of 1547, Lutheran leaders Philip of Hesse and Elector John Frederick of Saxony lost the war, surrendered, and became Charles' prisoners. This military defeat put the future of the Lutheran Reformation in a precarious situation across Germany, as Charles occupied many areas with imperial soldiers and had thoroughly defeated his main Protestant political rivals.

As challenging as this military loss was, an extra layer of conflict arose in the two halves of Saxony. There were two independent Saxon states, because in 1485 rule of the kingdom of Saxony had been divided between two brothers, Ernest and Albert. Albert's lands (Albertine Saxony) included the important cities of Dresden and Leipzig. Ernest received the electorship, an influential political status that gave Ernestine Saxony one of seven votes in the election of the Holy Roman emperors. Ernest's son Frederick the Wise established the University of Wittenberg in 1502 and protected Luther from the Edict of Worms. After Frederick died in 1525, the electorship went to his brother John and then his nephew John Frederick, both of whom strongly supported the Lutheran Reformation.

While Ernestine Saxony began reforming its churches in the 1520s, Albertine Saxony remained loyal to Rome under the rule of Frederick's cousin, Duke George. Not until after George's death in 1539 did his brother Heinrich introduce the Lutheran Reformation to that land. Heinrich's son Moritz continued the reform of churches in Albertine Saxony when he succeeded his father in 1541. Although Duke Moritz of Albertine Saxony and Elector John Frederick of Ernestine Saxony were Lutheran and were related to each other, they also stood as rival heads of state who nearly came to war over disputed territory in 1542.[8]

At the 1546 diet of Regensburg, Emperor Charles offered the electorship to Moritz—along with a verbal promise not to make religious changes—in exchange for Moritz's neutrality in the coming war against other Lutheran lands.[9] As the war proceeded, Moritz switched from neutrality to alliance with Charles and Charles' brother, King Ferdinand of Austria. As part of John Frederick's surrender in the spring of 1547, Charles transferred Wittenberg to Moritz's control and gave him the Saxon electorship as promised.

Moritz promptly supported the reopening of the University of Wittenberg, which had closed during the war. With the assurance that Moritz would allow them to teach and practice according to their Lutheran faith, leaders like Melanchthon, Bugenhagen, and other theologians decided to stay in Wittenberg with the people, churches and university that they had served for decades.[10]

Although Charles had verbally promised Moritz that the religious situation of his lands would not change after the Smalcaldic War, the victorious emperor put forth a document which would force Lutherans to return to the Church of Rome. Produced at the 1548 diet of Augsburg, this document came to be known as the Augsburg Interim, since it would be a temporary ("interim") religious policy until the Roman Catholic Council of Trent finished making its decrees and reforms, after which all German subjects would once again be brought into the faith and practice of the Church of Rome. Acknowledging that not all of the Protestant reforms could be immediately undone, the

8. Brecht, *Martin Luther: The Preservation of the Church, 1532–1546*, 292.
9. Martin Lohrmann, *Bugenhagen's Jonah: Biblical Interpretation as Public Theology* (Minneapolis: Lutheran University Press), 34.
10. Bugenhagen, *Selected Writings, Volume 1*, 163–64.

Interim made temporary concessions about the marriage of priests and the reception of both bread and wine by the laity in Holy Communion.[11] In some parts of Lutheran Germany, the Interim was enforced militarily, forcing church leaders like Nicholas von Amsdorf, Johannes Brenz, Martin Bucer, Nicholas Gallus, and Andreas Osiander to go into hiding or exile. Through a censorship clause, the Interim also made it a crime to publish critiques of this new religious policy.[12]

The situation in Moritz's Albertine Saxony grew extremely challenging, both politically and theologically.[13] Having received an early draft of the Interim from Moritz, Melanchthon and his colleagues were the first to write against it that spring.[14] Instead of either accepting or rejecting the document outright, Moritz stalled and looked for ways to avoid enforcing this deeply unpopular religious law in his lands. To do this, he brought together his political advisors, recently installed Catholic bishops, and Lutheran theologians like Melanchthon and other Wittenberg professors, who spent the next months attempting to craft an acceptable alternative.[15]

Although Charles finally appeared to have gained the upper hand over his Lutheran subjects, his victory in the Smalcaldic War ultimately led to his downfall. Dissatisfied with Charles's increased power, Moritz was able to organize and lead a successful coup against the emperor with the aid of other German princes and the king of France. In early 1552, their surprise military campaign made Lutheran lands free to restore their worship and reforms again. This legal allowance for territories to follow the faith of the *Augsburg Confession* within the Holy Roman Empire was enshrined in the 1555 Peace of Augsburg, which held until the start of the Thirty Years War in 1617.

By the time all these political events unfolded, however, many new controversies had come to dominate Lutheran church life. Those

---

11. Arand, Kolb, and Nestingen, 175–77.
12. Arand, Kolb, and Nestingen, 147.
13. For detailed studies of this subject, see Lohrmann, 36–48 and Arand, Kolb, and Nestingen, 179–83.
14. Timothy Wengert, "Not by Nature *Philoneikos*: Philip Melanchthon's Initial Reactions to the Augsburg Interim" in *Politik und Bekenntnis: Die Reaktionen auf das Interim von 1548*, eds. Irene Dingel and Günther Wartenberg (Leipzig: Evangelische Verlagsanstalt, 2006), 35.
15. Arand, Kolb, and Nestingen, 183–84.

outside of Moritz' newly-expanded lands accused the Wittenbergers of betraying Luther and the Reformation by working with Moritz and for not rebelling sufficiently against the Augsburg Interim. For their part, the Wittenberg theologians believed they had acted faithfully. They had bought in the negotiations and preserved their emphasis on justification by faith without provoking either a civil war or military reprisal from Charles. Lasting theological divisions arose from these conflicts, with lines mostly drawn between those who had worked with Melanchthon and those who agreed with leaders outside of Albertine Saxony like Nicholas von Amsdorf and Matthias Flacius Illyricus.[16]

## The Need for Harmony

In many ways, the *Augsburg Confession*'s assertion that unity in the gospel allowed for flexibility in local practices gave Lutherans a strong foundation for building up the church after the 1555 Peace of Augsburg. Lands that had been Lutheran before the Smalcaldic War again practiced as they had previously, using local church orders as the foundation for worship and teaching. But some critical points of tension remained.[17] The following two examples of conflict in the later 1550s serve as good illustrations of how disunity was harming Lutheran communities.

In 1556, King Ferdinand of Austria succeeded his brother Charles as Holy Roman Emperor. Ferdinand called for renewed dialogue between Catholic and Lutheran theologians, which took place in 1557 at the Colloquy of Worms. These talks, however, broke down: not because of differences between the Lutherans and Catholics, but because of disputes among the Lutherans that were based in the conflicts that arose during the Augsburg Interim years.[18]

Second, the following year, Melanchthon attempted to promote unity at an imperial gathering in Frankfurt. His efforts were again frustrated due to objections from theologians led by Flacius, who was

16. For more nuanced descriptions of these divisions, see Arand, Kolb, and Nestingen, 183–89.
17. For more detail on the historical and theological context of these years and their effect on the writing of the *Formula of Concord*, see Arand, Kolb, and Nestingen, 161–89 and 255–80.
18. Arand, Kolb, and Nestingen, 257.

then working in the rival state of Ernestine Saxony.[19] Such public disputes lent credence to critiques from Catholics and other Protestants that Lutheran theologians were fundamentally unable to agree with each other, let alone have constructive dialogue. In the face of these conflicts, *concordia* became an important value both for the sake of internal harmony and for witness to those of other religious persuasions.

An additional motive for internal harmony arose because of the Peace of Augsburg. This imperial settlement had legalized the faith of the *Augsburg Confession* but did not grant the same religious rights to lands that embraced Reformed or Calvinist beliefs. To get around this rule, Elector Frederick III of the Palatinate started to justify his land's Calvinist (more symbolic) interpretation of Holy Communion on the basis of a 1540 revision of the *Augsburg Confession* known as the *Variata*.[20] At the request of Elector John Frederick in 1540, Melanchthon had revised some articles of the *Augsburg Confession* in preparation for continued religious dialogue, including a revision of the article on the Lord's Supper. In 1561, Elector Frederick's Calvinist interpretation of the *Variata* prompted Lutherans to be more precise about their teaching of the Lord's Supper and about which edition of the *Augsburg Confession* to use. From this time onward, Lutherans would refer explicitly back to the "Unaltered Augsburg Confession" of 1530.

These controversies about Holy Communion reached a new peak in Albertine Saxony in the early 1570s: Moritz's brother and successor Elector August learned that his court theologians were secretly teaching his wife Calvinist ideas about the Lord's Supper, while telling her it was what Luther and Melanchthon had taught.[21] Enraged by their duplicity, August put the offending theologians in prison and supported efforts for Lutheran concord with new energy. To make many long stories short,[22] German Lutherans in the 1560s and 1570s

---

19. Arand, Kolb, and Nestingen, 258.
20. Arand, Kolb, and Nestingen, 174–75.
21. See Arand, Kolb, and Nestingen, 247–49.
22. For more detail on the historical and theological context of these years and their effect on the writing of the *Formula of Concord*, see Arand, Kolb, and Nestingen, 161–89 and 255–80.

had many reasons to seek concord and clearly express what they believed.

Jakob Andreae, a pastor and professor from Württemberg in southwestern Germany, came close to providing a basis for unity with a 1573 collection of sermons, the full title of which reads, *Six Christian Sermons on the Divisions among the Theologians of the Augsburg Confession, How a Simple Pastor and a Common Christian Layperson Should Deal with Them on the Basis of the Catechism.*[23] In line with the early Reformation's care for teaching the faith in simple ways, Andreae chose to frame the issues in ways that ordinary pastors and parishioners would understand. To do this, he built his work on Luther's catechism and wrote accessible sermons rather than complex theological treatises.

Andreae sent his *Six Christian Sermons* to colleagues around Germany, including other second-generation leaders like Martin Chemnitz and David Chytraeus. Chemnitz was a highly-respected voice among those who had generally been critical of the Wittenberg theologians after the Augsburg Interim, while Chytraeus represented a moderate Melanchthonian perspective. For the sake of clarity, Chemnitz and Chytraeus suggested that Andreae rewrite the *Six Christian Sermons* as more formal doctrinal statements. After Andreae did this, they revised it further and sent their work to other theologians who similarly represented different regions and perspectives. As the document got longer and more complicated, politicians asked for a shorter edition. Andreae obliged by writing the *Epitome of the Formula of Concord*, which explained each of the disputed topics as a list of theses and antitheses (*pro* and *contra* statements).

In light of such cooperation, the *Formula of Concord* represents a high level of communal consensus. The theologians were careful to represent differing positions accurately and to be clear about what they meant and what they did not mean. Fascinating insights into the composition of the *Formula of Concord* have come to us through the work of George Fritschel (one of my predecessors at Wartburg

23. For commentary on and translation of these sermons, see Robert Kolb, *Andreae and the Formula of Concord* (St. Louis: Concordia, 1977).

Seminary). About one hundred years ago, Dr. Fritschel compared the various drafts of the *Formula* in order to identify who wrote each section; from his efforts we can see where writers would sometimes add important clarifications one paragraph or one sentence at a time. Fritschel's efforts highlight the collaborative nature of the *Formula of Concord* and show how its writers used each other's strengths to reach agreement, traits that we will examine below.

Most of all, the *Formula*'s authors hoped to clarify the gospel message of reconciliation through Christ without adding something new to it. The heading given to the Epitome, for instance, introduces the work as:

> A THOROUGH, CLEAR, CORRECT
> and Final Repetition and Explanation of Certain Articles of the
> Augsburg Confession on Which Controversy Has Arisen for a Time
> among Certain Theologians Adhering to This Confession,
> Resolved and Settled according to the Direction of God's Word
> and the Summary Formulation of Our Christian Teaching[24]

The formality of this description should not overshadow its main points. These church leaders wanted to explain their biblical faith in a way that clarified—not added to—the articles of the *Augsburg Confession*. Recognizing that the conflicts of the previous decades called for a clear confession of faith, they affirmed the *Augsburg Confession* as fitting the needs of their context, calling it "our creed for this age" even as they sought to settle new issues in relevant ways.[25]

## Spirit and Service in the Formula

Through its methods of clear language, dialogue, and consensus, the *Formula* addressed controversial points by identifying main issues, clarifying terms, and explaining why certain views ought to be accepted or rejected. In all this, the spiritual concern that people hear, receive and share the good news of Jesus Christ remained central.

The *Formula*'s first article, for instance, concerns original sin. In order to emphasize how much people need the truly amazing grace of

---

24. Ep 486. The Solid Declaration begins with a nearly identical heading, SD 524.
25. SD 527.

God, theologians like Flacius taught a strong doctrine of original sin: without God, humans are absolutely and utterly lost.[26] While this in itself was not controversial and followed the teachings of the *Augustana* and its *Apology*, conflicts arose when it came to wondering how sin entered human life. Had God done a bad or incomplete job of creating humans? Was corrupted and sinful human nature put there by the devil, making humanity creatures of the devil rather than a loving God? The authors of the *Formula* carefully parsed these questions, discussed relevant scriptural passages and considered the theological and practical implications of these ideas.

In the case of original sin, this meant emphasizing the good news that people were created by a good and loving God and are not creatures of the devil. Referring to the lumps of clay [*massa* in Latin] from which humans were formed in Gen 2:7, Chemnitz wrote, "Here upright Christian hearts should remember the indescribable goodness of God, that God does not cast such a corrupted, perverted, sinful *massa* [lump of clay] immediately into the fires of hell. Instead, out of it God makes and fashions human nature as it now is, so tragically corrupted by sin, so that he might cleanse, sanctify, and save it through his dear Son."[27] Acknowledging that human nature had become corrupted material because of sin, Chemnitz explained that God did not abandon or disown our sinful reality but remained an active, hands-on creator both before and after sin entered the world.

To this image from Genesis 2 Chemnitz added further biblical language of God as a good potter who shapes the lives not of idealized saints but real people with real problems, invoking—among other passages—the prophet Isaiah's words about his beloved yet stumbling people, "Yet, O Lord, you are our Father; we are the clay, and you are our potter; we are all the work of your hand" (Isa 64:8).[28] While the *Formula*'s discussion of original sin justifiably included philosophical

---

26. For more on Flacius' theology, see Luka Ilić, *Theologian of Sin and Grace: The Process of Radicalization in the Theology of Matthias Flacius Illyricus* (Göttingen: Vandenhoek & Ruprecht, 2014), especially chapter 3.
27. SD 538.39.
28. SD 537.34.

and theological ideas about human nature and the origins of evil, Chemnitz brought his focus back to basic spiritual and personal realities: even when they feel far from God, "upright Christian hearts" should not worry that God does not know them, love them, or care about them; instead, people can be confident that God continues to shape them in life-giving ways.

Controversies on free will and good works similarly received treatment through this method of identifying the main concerns, rejecting extreme positions, and refocusing on the personal reception of God's grace. Because debates about good works and free will mostly revolved around theologians influenced by Melanchthon, David Chytraeus served as the primary writer of these sections, giving balanced explanations to the various perspectives.

The question of free will, for instance, revisited the central idea of the early Reformation that humans do not contribute to their own salvation. At the same time, Melanchthon and his students wanted to say that people are not inert "blocks of wood" that have no will of their own, either before or after justification. In his efforts to clarify this issue, Chytraeus affirmed that God alone saves and that salvation comes from God alone when the Holy Spirit works through law and gospel in Christian preaching.[29] He also referred to Luther's teaching that people are entirely passive when it comes to being converted to God.[30]

But if all this happens externally, with no human participation, where is God in the hearts and minds of believers? To address this concern, Chytraeus cited St. Paul to discuss the great comfort Christians can have about God's work in their lives, including in their minds.

Paul wrote in Philippians 2[:13]: "For it is God who is at work in you, enabling you both to will and to work for his good pleasure." This precious verse is very comforting for all pious Christians who feel and perceive a tiny glimmer and longing for God's grace and eternal salvation in their hearts. For they know that God has ignited this beginning of true

29. See especially SD 553.48–554.46.
30. SD 561.89.

godliness in their hearts and, moreover, that he wants to strengthen them in their great weakness and help them, so that they may persevere in true faith to the end.[31]

Though people cannot make themselves holy or grow in holiness through their own efforts, they can trust that God will and does work in them: after all, God does not convert mindless blocks of wood but converts real human hearts and minds. Chytraeus added that whatever good happens in believers "occurs not on the basis of our fleshly, natural powers but on the basis of the new powers and gifts which the Holy Spirit initiated in us in conversion. . . . This should be understood in no other way than that the converted do good to the extent that God rules, leads, and guides them with his Holy Spirit."[32] Here the *Formula of Concord* balanced care that people really know that the Holy Spirit is at work in them with the assertion that selfless good works come not from our best efforts or good intentions but entirely as gifts of God.

When it came to the article on good works, the writers of the *Formula* had to address the proposition that "good words are necessary for salvation." Especially important here was the recognition that the word "necessary" can mean two different things: on one hand, good works being necessary can mean that they inevitably (necessarily) follow a justified life; on the other, it can mean that good works are a precondition (necessity) for salvation, a position that Lutherans steadfastly rejected.

To emphasize the importance of good works as a fruit of faith and not as a cause of salvation, the *Formula* cited extensively from Martin Luther's preface to Romans:

> Faith is a divine work in us which changes us and makes us to be born anew of God. It kills the old "Adam" and makes us altogether different people, in heart and spirit and mind and all powers; and it brings with it the Holy Spirit. O, it is a living, busy, active, mighty thing, this faith. It is impossible for it not to be doing good works incessantly . . . Faith is a living, daring confidence in God's grace, so sure and certain that the believer will stake life itself on it a thousand times.[33]

31. SD 546.14.
32. SD 556.65-66.

Once again, the reformers emphasized the lively power of faith to change believers and the world through confidence in God's love and mercy. This biblical and practical concern for spiritual truth and concrete works of service continuously shines through, even as the *Formula of Concord* often used technical theological language and concepts to address the conflicts of the time. Adding quotations from a cherished work like Luther's preface to Romans further served to advance mutual understanding and harmony.

### Christ's Real Presence

In addition to questions about human nature like original sin and free will, the writers of the *Formula of Concord* also focused on Christ's presence in the world, especially in the sacrament of the Lord's Supper. If—as Christians confess in the Apostles' Creed—Jesus Christ "ascended into heaven" and "is seated at the right hand of the Father," how could he be physically present in the bread and wine of Holy Communion?

Martin Luther had debated Christ's real presence with other Protestants like Huldrych Zwingli already in the 1520s. At the Marburg Colloquy of 1529, these reformers gathered together, agreeing that "the Sacrament of the Altar is a sacrament of the true body and blood of Jesus Christ, and the spiritual reception of this body and blood is particularly necessary for every Christian."[34] And yet, even as they agreed on the importance of communion, they had to conclude: "we have not at this time agreed whether the true body and blood of Christ are bodily in the bread and wine."[35] Different ways of interpreting the biblical texts about Holy Communion combined with different ideas about the primary importance of the sacrament for Christian life to produce this impasse.

Zwingli's side took the statement that Christ ascended to "the right hand of the Father" (as in Acts 2:33) literally. With his body in heaven, this would mean that Jesus Christ cannot also be physically present

---

33. SD 576.10-12, citing LW 35:370-371.
34. Arand, Kolb, and Nestingen, 91.
35. Ibid.

on earth. At the same time, Zwingli believed that the words "this is my body" and "this is my blood" (Matt 26:26-27) should not be taken literally but refer to Christ's promise to be spiritually present to believers.[36]

The Lutherans believed the opposite. First, they interpreted the statement that Christ "is seated at the right hand of the Father" figuratively, with the understanding that "the right hand of God" is a common biblical metaphor for God's power.[37] In that case, Christ's physical body is one with the almighty and omnipresent Lord of creation. If the fully human Christ is one with the power of God, then Christ's resurrected and ascended body can be physically present whenever and wherever God wills. Therefore, they found no reason why Christians should not interpret the words "this is my body" to mean what they say: Christ's presence in communion is founded upon the reliable word of the one who has promised to be there. As Lutheran historian Timothy Wengert has put it, "When Jesus throws a party, he shows up."[38] In this way, Christ's presence in the sacrament embodies God's promises and presence to the flesh-and-blood people who need such divine aid.

While the Lutheran and Zwinglian Reformations shared much in common, finding agreement on this particular point proved elusive. This remained true, despite later attempts like the 1536 *Wittenberg Concord* in which the Lutherans and south German reformers temporarily agreed on a shared view of Holy Communion. John Calvin's language of a "spiritual eating" further complicated rather than clarified the discussion.[39] At the great cost of division among otherwise sympathetic sides of the Reformation, what spiritual reasons did the Lutherans have for insisting so fiercely on Christ's physical presence in the Lord's Supper which other Protestants found objectionable?

In a word: assurance. At the risk of division with other Protestants,

36. A summary of this view is given by the authors of the *Formula of Concord* in SD 592.2–594.7.
37. LW 37:68.
38. Timothy Wengert, *A Formula for Parish Practice: Using the Formula of Concord in Congregations* (Grand Rapids, MI: Eerdmans, 2006), 103.
39. John Calvin, *Institutes of the Christian Religion*, volume 2, edited by John T. McNeil (Philadelphia: Westminster, 1960), book 4, chapter 17, especially 1403-1411.

Lutherans viewed the sacrament as a tangible way to receive the gospel message of God who set aside godliness in order to restore a broken world. Because of sin in ourselves and in the world around us, there are always ample reasons to doubt this good news and the spiritual reality of grace and reconciliation. Precisely because of our creaturely weakness and doubts, however, Christ gave this creaturely means of grace, so that sinners can know, experience and taste the truth of this message in their own bodies. As Chytraeus put it in the *Formula*, "all who eat and drink the consecrated bread and wine in the Supper receive and partake of the true, essential body and blood of Christ orally. Believers receive it as a certain pledge and assurance that their sins are truly forgiven and that Christ dwells in them with his power."[40]

Here the *Formula* follows the pattern we saw repeated in Luther and Melanchthon's works: it identifies what a thing is and what a thing does. The teaching about what Christ's presence is informs what the sacrament does: it gives the saving presence of Christ who forgives sins and gives the new life of God. Further, just as Luther stressed that this sacrament is for those who really need God's help to trust and serve as we ought, Chytraeus added:

> The true and worthy guests, for whom this precious sacrament above all was instituted and established, are the Christians who are weak in faith, fragile and troubled, who are terrified in their hearts by the immensity and number of their sins and think that they are not worthy of this precious treasure and of the benefits of Christ because of their great impurity, who feel the weakness of their faith and deplore it, and who desire with all their heart to serve God with a stronger, more resolute faith and purer obedience.[41]

Once again, theological concerns revolved around care for those who are "weak in faith, fragile and troubled;" in short, for real people. To show that the Lutherans aimed for biblical faithfulness, the *Formula* then cited several New Testament verses about Christ coming precisely for the sake of the weak, for instance, "Come to me, all you that are weary and are carrying heavy burdens, and I will give you rest" (Matt

40. SD 604.63.
41. SD 605.69.

11:28) and "God's power is made mighty in the weak" (2 Cor 12:9).[42] Far from getting lost in formalized doctrinal systems, the evangelical message of the early Reformation remained central for the second generation of Lutheran reformers and communities.

A similarly passionate insistence upon Christ's radical work of giving everything in order to reclaim the lost and the weak appears in the *Formula*'s article on Christ's descent to hell. While this doctrine had not inspired a large controversy, theologians had different ideas about what it meant that Christ descended to the dead: Did Christ descend in body, in spirit, or both? Was this descent a part of his suffering or his glorification?[43] Though its place in the Apostles' Creed (on the basis of verses like 1 Pet 3:19, 1 Pet 4:6 and Eph 4:8-10) gives it a prominent place in Christian faith, this line may still appear to be an obscure point to focus on. Looking to prevent unhelpful speculation and advance people's understanding of the gospel message, the Lutheran reformers lifted up this topic as a moving description of the great depths to which God will go to save us: however one understands it, God has gone through death and hell to reclaim the lost. Saying little about this teaching itself, the *Formula* instead referred readers to a sermon that Luther gave on this topic in 1533. There Luther preached,

> Neither hell nor the devil can take us and all others who believe on him captive nor can they do us harm . . . Those who say the Creed and cling to it shall follow after, for Christ has gone before us that we should follow after him. He has initiated this so that we might daily rise in him through the Word and Baptism.[44]

The creed's words about Christ's descent to the dead promises that Christians can be confident there is nowhere in creation we can go where Christ is not able to save. There is no place or no situation, including the hell and darkness of death itself, where Christ cannot reach us. Those who confess the creed during worship and in personal prayer get to claim this wonderful promise for themselves every day.

---

42. SD 605.70f.
43. BC 634, footnote 305.
44. Arand, Kolb, and Nestingen, 249 and 252.

Further, in his typical way, Luther connected this good news with the Holy Spirit's down-to-earth activity in the church's ministry of word and sacraments: Christ "has initiated this so that we might daily rise in him through the Word and Baptism."

## The Comforting Doctrine of Predestination

The doctrine of election (also called predestination) considers God's eternal knowledge about who will be saved. Lutherans had discussed this biblical concept in works like Melanchthon's 1521 *Loci Communes* and Luther's 1525 *Bondage of the Will*. Mostly, however, they were content to let divine omniscience remain a mystery that belongs to God and not to people. Melanchthon, for instance, had advised, "We do better to adore the mysteries of Deity than to investigate them."[45] Luther likewise let the mysteries of God's election serve as a path that leads doubting hearts to faith:

> As long as [a person] is persuaded that he himself can do even the least thing toward his salvation, he retains some self-confidence and does not altogether despair of himself, and therefore he is not humbled before God, but presumes that there is—or at least hopes or desires that there may be—some place, time, and work for him, by which he may at length attain to salvation. But when a man has no doubt that everything depends on the will of God, then he completely despairs of himself and chooses nothing for himself, but waits for God to work; then he has come close to grace, and can be saved. It is thus for the sake of the elect that these things are published, in order that being humbled and brought back to nothingness by this means they may be saved.[46]

For the Lutheran reformers, the good news in the doctrine of predestination is that God has mysteriously chosen sinners for salvation, without regard to their works or worthiness. While the idea that God knows in advance who will be saved might lead people to despair because of their unworthiness, it most of all ought to remind sinners of the entirely unconditional goodness of a God who loves them and who has given this gospel promise to all nations. In short,

45. *Loci Communes*, 21.
46. LW 33:62.

Lutherans understood worrying about predestination to be part of the Holy Spirit's work of leading people to faith through law and gospel: despairing of our own human righteousness, we turn to God alone for forgiveness, life, and love.

While Lutherans had preferred to let the question of "who is saved" remain a mystery, stressing instead God's promises to all who believe, Geneva reformer John Calvin went further than this when he discussed predestination in his influential *Institutes of the Christian Religion.* If God knows all things and knows who will be saved, Calvin reasoned, then God also knows who will *not* be saved in the Last Judgment. Calvin then asserted that since the Bible discusses the issue that some are not saved, this, too, must be a valid topic for Christians to consider. "For Scripture is the school of the Holy Spirit, in which, as nothing is omitted that is both necessary and useful to know, so nothing is taught but what is expedient to know."[47] Unlike the Lutherans, Calvin thought it was important to consider what it means that some people are destined for eternal condemnation.

This focus on some being saved and some being damned has come to be called "double predestination." As Calvin described it, "We call predestination God's eternal decree, by which he compacted with himself what he will to become of each man. For all are not created in equal condition; rather, eternal life is foreordained for some, eternal damnation for others."[48] In the same way as the Lutherans, Calvin explored this teaching in order to emphasize the total extent to which salvation is an entirely free gift of God, unrelated to human works. He, too, taught that scripture gave this teaching in order that, "humbled and cast down, we may learn to tremble at [God's] judgment and esteem his mercy."[49]

Lutherans, however, objected to double predestination. They did so not because it was illogical or unscriptural, but because it seemed to work against the church's main practical task of announcing the good news that God extends salvation to all. Rather than leaving people

47. *Institutes of the Christian Religion*, 2:924.
48. *Institutes of the Christian Religion*, 2:926.
49. *Institutes of the Christian Religion*, 2:960.

144

to wonder which category they were in, Lutherans taught a "single predestination" (sometimes called a "broken" predestination), in which those who wonder if God wants to save them can trust that the answer is yes: on the basis of God's gospel promises given to all peoples and all creation, there is never a need to doubt that God is ultimately for us and our salvation.

For this reason, the *Epitome of the Formula of Concord* calls its teaching about predestination "an article of comfort when properly treated."[50] Wanting to avoid the doubts that can come when wondering about God's eternal plan for individual lives, the Lutherans rested their faith on the word of promise given freely to all through gospel preaching, ministry and service.

In passages mostly written by Martin Chemnitz, the *Formula* teaches the many comforts that come from knowing that God has desired and worked for salvation from the beginning of time. Similarly, because God's promises are trustworthy and effective, knowing God's intention to save "gives us wonderful comfort in crosses and trials, that in his counsel before time began God determined and decreed that he would stand by us in every trouble, grant us patience, give us comfort, create hope and provide a way out of all things so that we may be saved [cf. 1 Cor 10:13]."[51] This perspective teaches that we do not endure troubles and trials on our own but can have the confidence that our suffering conforms to the cross of Christ: suffering and death will be transformed into life. Citing Romans 8, Chemnitz added, "the cross of each should and must 'work together for the good' of that person."[52]

A constant temptation, of course, is to want to know more than God has revealed. In light of this, the *Formula* recommended that we always consider predestination in light of Christ's saving action for all and the promises of scripture. But of all the words in the Bible about the will of God, which scriptures should people turn to when considering the mystery of God's eternal election? Andreae put it simply when he wrote,

50. Ep 517.1.
51. SD 648.48.
52. SD 648.49, citing Rom 8:28.

Therefore, if people wish to be saved, they should not concern or torture themselves with thoughts about the secret counsel of God . . . Rather, they should listen to Christ, who is the 'Book of Life' and the book of God's eternal election for all God's children to eternal life [Phil 4:3; Rev. 3:5; 20:15]. For he testifies to all people without distinction that God wills all people who are burdened and weighed down with sins to come to him, so that they may be given rest and be saved [Matt 11:28].[53]

Describing a faith in God that recalls Luther's early struggles with the righteousness of God, the writers of the Formula taught that doubts about salvation and grace need not ultimately be signs of God's disfavor; instead, even doubts, struggles and temptations can become new opportunities to turn to Christ for life.[54] On this point, the Formula again turned to scripture and Luther's preface to Romans:

We should therefore not attempt to fathom the abyss of God's hidden foreknowledge, as it is written in Luke 13[:23, 24]. When someone asked, "Lord, do you think that only a few will be saved?" Christ answered, "Strive to enter through the narrow door." Thus, Luther says, "Follow the order of the Epistle to the Romans. Worry first about Christ and the gospel, that you may recognize your sin and his grace, and then fight your sin, as Paul teaches from the first to the eighth chapters. Then, when you come under the cross and suffering in the eighth chapter, this will teach you of foreknowledge in chapters 9, 10, and 11, and how comforting it is."[55]

As this section comes to its close, the Formula's teaching about predestination does not leave people to wonder about God's grace or to assume that the life of God's elect is a straight and easy path. "Instead, it leads poor sinners to true, proper repentance, raises them up through faith, strengthens them in new obedience, and thus justifies and saves them eternally, solely through the merit of Christ."[56] Engaging an important theological issue of their time, this article on God's eternal election shows how the second generation of Lutherans kept their focus on law and gospel, sharing the personal comfort of the gospel, and encouraging lives of faith one day at a time.

53. SD 651.70.
54. SD 655.89.
55. SD 646.33, citing LW 35:378.
56. SD 655.96f.

146

## Conclusion

The *Formula of Concord* richly examined the issues confronting Lutheran communities more than half a century after Luther's *95 Theses* started the Reformation. Although the *Formula* offers many other fascinating things to teach beyond what has been discussed here, this chapter has focused on showing that the early Luther's evangelical message of justification by faith alone remained central to the second generation of church leaders. As in the confessional writings of Luther and Melanchthon, the *Formula of Concord* sought to clarify the spiritual treasure of the gospel so that people can know and apply its benefits in daily life.

Beyond the theologians who worked on the *Formula* and the more than eight thousand pastors who affirmed its teaching, the political leaders of the time expressed their hope that this document and its 1580 publication with the other documents in the *Book of Concord* would serve both personal faith and love of neighbor. Signing their names to the preface written by Jakob Andreae and Martin Chemnitz, these princes and city councils affirmed that this expression of Christian faith would serve them "in the promotion of God's glory and of the common welfare, both eternal and temporal."[57] Although one may wonder if politicians said such things cynically as a cover for increased power and influence, the conflicts of the previous decades had created significant obstacles to stability and peace. Seeking a more lasting harmony for both spiritual and practical reasons, these leaders pledged their desire to live according to the teachings explained in the *Book of Concord* as part of what it meant for them to "live in genuine peace and unity" as members of a diverse political body like the Holy Roman Empire.[58] From imperial gatherings to local parishes, the heart of all these efforts remained the conviction that faith in Christ fills individual lives with grace and inspires people to serve each other in socially and spiritually enriching ways.

57. BC 15.22.
58. BC 15.23.

# Epilogue: The Lifelong Adventure of Faith

## Reprise: Why Reformation History?

I started this book with a story about an early time in my life when Reformation history affected my relationship with my best friend. Over the years, I have continued to learn more about religion and religious history, always discovering fascinating ways in which faith and daily life inform and interact with each other.

In my own experience as a practicing Lutheran and student of history, asking hard questions has repeatedly led me to new learning about myself, Christianity, and the world around me. When I have wondered about the existence of God, Luther's explanation to the first commandment has continued to open doors about who God is (and is not). When I ponder the divinity of Christ, the theology of the cross testifies to the greatness of a God who became one with our flesh and even went through death to give life. And when it comes to wondering what difference faith makes in the real world, it becomes increasingly apparent that the world needs love: not the easy kind of love that feels good for a while but the deep love that comes from learning what it means to trust God above all else and to love our neighbors as ourselves. This is also a love that does not pretend we can be purer, holier or more ethical, if only we tried, worked or loved harder; instead, this is a love aimed right at our mixed-up, imperfect, flesh-and-blood realities.

A life in the church has put me in contact with other Lutherans from around the world, with other Christians in the places I have lived, and with people of other faiths. I also enjoy talking about Christian faith in various ways with people who do not consider themselves religious or identify with specific religious communities. These encounters have taught me the joy that comes with practicing the Golden Rule: "in everything, do to others as you would have them do to you" (Matt 7:12). I can claim and share my own faith, even as I practice the respectful conversations and behavior that I would want to receive from others. Love of my own tradition has taught me to see how and why others love and cherish their religious and cultural heritages, as well. The "love and zeal for the truth" that inspired Luther has also motivated me to keep learning new things, from the natural sciences and economics to the arts and philosophy. Love for the truth also provides a way from within the tradition to practice necessary criticism of the tradition. In short, the "love and zeal for the truth" that introduced Luther's 95 Theses remains a great starting point for our contemporary quests for meaning, goodness and grace.

This book has sought to highlight positive aspects of the Lutheran confessional tradition; Lutheranism still has much to teach people who are interested in learning from it. This effort to identify positive aspects has not been done naively. Luther could be boorish. Melanchthon could be aloof. Their colleagues and successors often lost sight of liberating gospel faith and let doctrinal arguments or worldly wisdom get in the way of being theologians of the cross. Although freedom was a major goal of the Reformation, Christians of the time often uncritically accepted what we would now call patriarchal and Eurocentric views of the world. As my church youth director once told us, Lutherans have plenty of skeletons in the closet. These include participation in misuse of the environment, colonialism, racism, and the Holocaust. Like the disciples who betrayed or fled Jesus at the time of his arrest, Lutherans have found many ways to avoid the cross and hurt others, rather than help them.

As with those first disciples, however, our failures do not need to be the end of the story. Christ continues to walk through locked doors to strengthen weak and fearful people through the free gift of reconciliation and the life-giving presence of the Holy Spirit. If the Lutheran branch of Christianity remains compelling, it is not for its own sake, but in the way that it keeps pointing to a Lord who goes through death and hell to save the lost. With historical roots in sustained questions of identity, repentance and liberation, Lutheranism offers an extended, experiential meditation on what it means to live into Jesus' words, "The time is fulfilled and the kingdom of God has come near; repent, and believe in the good news" (Mark 1:15). God willing, within the one church of Christ, Lutherans around the world will continue to have unique ways of showing what daily repentance and rising with Christ can look like.

## Faith as a Lifelong Adventure

This daily dying and rising is an adventure for a lifetime. In his book *Fear and Trembling*, Søren Kierkegaard gave a great reflection on the fact that faith is not something easily mastered but involves a lifelong journey with God. Having studied for the ministry before committing himself to writing, Kierkegaard described faith in ways that challenged his contemporaries in the nineteenth-century Danish Lutheran church, who had too-often come to value reasonability and respectability more than the adventure of faith. In the preface to *Fear and Trembling*, Kierkegaard's fictional author Johannes de Silentio asked his peers where they were going in life that they could so quickly leave faith behind in favor of more enlightened and sophisticated pursuits. Johannes observed:

> In our age, everyone is unwilling to stop with faith but goes further. It perhaps would be rash to ask where they are going, whereas it is a sign of urbanity and culture for me to assume that everyone has faith, since otherwise it certainly would be odd to speak of going further. It was different in those ancient days. Faith was then a task for a whole lifetime, because it was assumed that proficiency in believing is not acquired either in days or weeks.[1]

1. Søren Kiekegaard, *Fear and Trembling/Repetition*, edited and translated by Howard Hong and Edna Hong (Princeton: Princeton, 1983), 7.

Through the eyes of Johannes de Silentio, *Fear and Trembling* then considers how hard it is really to trust God with all one's being. The enigmatic story of Abraham's near-sacrifice of his beloved son Isaac from Genesis 22 serves as the catalyst for this meditation on faith. In the end, Johannes concludes that faith is not something that one can go beyond. Instead, "the person who has come to faith (whether he is extraordinarily gifted or plain and simple does not matter) does not come to a standstill in faith. Indeed, he would be indignant if anyone said this to him, just as the lover would resent it if someone said that he came to a standstill in love; for, he would answer, I am by no means standing still. I have my whole life in it."[2]

Here Kierkegaard's ficitious author points out that faith is as endless as love. It is also worth noting that Johannes de Silential praises faith in people who might be considered either extraordinary or simple. In faith, the usual worldly categories or criteria for worthiness, giftedness, or ability do not apply. As Jesus said about the children who gathered around him, "Let the little children come to me, and do not stop them; for it is to such as these that the kingdom of heaven belongs" (Matt 19:14). Faith and Christian wisdom belong to everyone.

Intentionally or not, the description of faith as a lifelong adventure in *Fear and Trembling* echoes Luther's opening words in *The Freedom of a Christian*:

> Many people view the Christian faith as something easy, and some even place it among the virtues. They do this because they have not experienced faith, nor have they tasted its great power. A person must experience the strength faith provides in the midst of trials and misfortune. Otherwise, it is not possible to write well about faith or to understand what has been written about it. But one who has had even a small taste of faith can never write, speak, reflect, or hear enough concerning it. As Christ says, it is a "spring of water welling up to eternal life" (John 4:14).[3]

This conviction—that Christian faith is a lifelong adventure with God—propelled much of the Lutheran Reformation, though it is by

---

2. *Fear and Trembling*, 122–23.
3. *The Freedom of a Christian*, 49; cf. LW 31:343.

no means unique to Lutheranism. Already in the first decades of the church, the Acts of the Apostles described early believers as those who belonged to the Way, people on a Holy Spirit-filled journey with God through Christ.[4] Medieval theologians described the Christian as a *viator* (a traveler or pilgrim),[5] as did the English Puritan John Bunyan in his classic *The Pilgrim's Progress* from the late 1600s, and African-American Christians in spirituals like "I Want Jesus to Walk with Me." This shared understanding of faith as a journey connects many branches of the Christian tradition that have developed in otherwise distinctive ways.

In "here I stand" moments like Luther's trial at the Diet of Worms and the presentation of the *Augsburg Confession*, the Lutheran reformers expressed precisely this desire to remain within the "one, holy, catholic, and apostolic church." At the same time, their accents on justification by faith alone, on Christians as "simultaneously righteous and sinner," and on the lifelong encounter with God's word as law and gospel eventually did give shape to a unique Christian path, whether due to sharp conflicts or through new ways of living into the teaching of justification by faith alone.

This book has attempted to lift up spiritual and practical insights of the Lutheran Reformation, many of which remain inspiring and valuable in the early twenty-first century. Most of all, I hope that readers have a good sense of the Reformation's core focus on the gospel message of forgiveness, reconciliation, love and new life given freely by God through the person of Jesus Christ. While Luther himself is a fascinating character for many reasons, his concern was not about himself but about sharing the gospel as a source of life. As he wrote in the explanation to the Apostles' Creed, "I believe that Jesus Christ ... is my Lord."[6] The "I" in that sentence does not belong to Luther but to every person who enters into the endlessly fascinating, challenging, and life-giving Way of Jesus Christ.

---

4. Acts 9:2, 19:9, 19:23, and 22:4.
5. As in Heiko Oberman, *The Harvest of Medieval Theology* (Cambridge, MA: Harvard, 1963), 39.
6. SC 355.4; see also chapter 3.

## The Adventurous Faith of the Lutheran Confessions

How did the works that make up the *Book of Concord* express this adventurous faith? In a course that I once team-taught on Luther's catechisms and social media, our class studied the catechism as a kind of "platform" or operating system more than as a simple set of answers. And indeed, Luther's catechisms present the Ten Commandments, the Apostles' Creed, the Lord's Prayer, and the sacraments in ways that encourage us to view them as the building blocks of faith for life in a complex world. The question of whether or not the Lutheran Confessions as a whole, however, encourage such a view has generally received less attention.

This is especially true because the person who contributed the most pages to the *Book of Concord*, Philip Melanchthon, has been much maligned over the centuries. Lutherans have tended to undervalue him as a second-tier reformer and as one who was perhaps too quick to depart from Luther's formulations, while non-Lutherans have overlooked him precisely because of his deep participation in the Lutheran Reformation. He has been accused of over-systematizing the faith, on one hand, and of not sufficiently understanding the gospel, on the other. This unfortunate impression needs to be corrected, since Melanchthon's writings show him to be deeply and personally familiar with the gospel theology he and Luther taught together for decades. We still have many things to learn from this Renaissance scholar who engaged the world around him in exciting ways, and whose expertise included not only theology and classical languages but the natural sciences, political theory, history, and educational reform.

Uncertainty about Melanchthon has sometimes kept Lutherans from fully grasping their own central writings. The *Augsburg Confession*, for instance, can be criticized today for being either too interested in Christian unity or too particular to Lutheran theology. For the Lutherans of its time (including Luther), it satisfactorily balanced both sides, expressing the reformers' catholicity even as it described the reforms of teaching, worship and daily life that had led to conflicts with Rome. Similarly, the *Apology of the Augsburg Confession* stands as a masterful piece of technical theological writing as well as an impassioned work of spiritual care. In it, Melanchthon used rich language like "personal faith," the "benefits of Christ," and the church as "an association of faith and the Holy Spirit in the hearts of believers." Melanchthon dedicated his life to seeking and sharing the truth of the gospel for the sake of individuals and communities, a legacy worth claiming and cherishing. His emphasis on "what a thing is" and "what a thing does" remains a powerful way to approach faith in terms of identity and effects.

Luther's *Smalcald Articles* likewise offer a confessional corrective to the stereotype that the later reformer had lost the spirit of his earlier career. These articles do this by focusing on gospel freedom and Christian service. How can both be promoted without going too far in either direction? Luther's answer is to live by faith, trust God, and be ready to watch the Holy Spirit work in, around and through us. Amid deep conflicts with the institutional church, Luther tried to keep things simple: "God be praised, a seven-year-old child knows what the church is: holy believers and 'the little sheep who hear the voice of their shepherd.'"[7] Rather than presenting an arid theological system, the *Smalcald Articles* show Luther passionately sharing the liberating gospel message that started the Reformation in the first place.

Finally, despite needing to address decades-old theological disputes on more complicated levels, the *Formula of Concord* also continued to value a faith that made sense for ordinary people and that served real communities. As in Luther and Melanchthon's work, the *Formula* uses language about human hearts, comfort, personal faith, and embodied experiences of the gospel. More than just a cynical word to use in quests to centralize religious or social power, "harmony" mattered to the second generation of Lutherans because it had been sorely lacking. Concord was itself a blessed effect of the gospel to be earnestly desired when absent and to be cherished when experienced. The collaborative and collegial way that the *Formula* was written over years to span

7. SA 324.2.

155

geographical, political and theological distances testifies to this appreciation for harmony and dialogue.

Do these things still speak to people in the early twenty-first century? As a parish pastor curious to find out, I once dedicated one autumn of my congregation's adult education time to a study of the *Augsburg Confession*. I planned to spend each session discussing one or two articles, giving just enough background information for people to understand the general context. Aside from that, we would simply read an article or two and discuss it. Since the *Augsburg Confession* begins with articles on God, original sin, Jesus Christ, justification, preaching, and good works, I figured that if we couldn't get thirty or forty minutes of conversation on these topics, then we had deeper problems to worry about.

As it happened, these topics and the ways the *Augsburg Confession* presented them fascinated our class. We discussed who God is, what it means to believe that humans are born sinful, and what it means to need a savior. We considered the biblical ideas behind these and many other teachings. It was in this class, too, that a member of my church observed how much the Holy Spirit appears in the text, even though there is no separate article on the Spirit. People brought their questions and together we learned more about the church's spiritual heritage, our community of believers and each other. In short, I discovered that the answer was a clear yes: the *Augsburg Confession* explains Christian faith in fascinating, sensible, and useful ways for people today. Without itself being sacred scripture, it does a remarkable job of discussing the whats and the wherefores of the gospel.

For those who would like to read more about how Lutheran Christians have engaged their world to make a difference, I recommend starting with the following recent autobiographies by Lutheran leaders. First, Heidi Neumark's book *Breathing Space: A Spiritual Journey in the South Bronx* relates her work with the people of Transfiguration Lutheran Church to care for their neighborhood and each other; in *Hidden Inheritance: Family Secrets, Memory, and Faith*

Neumark examines her family history to wrestle with questions of faith and the Holocaust.[8] Next, Leymah Gbowee's *Mighty Be Our Powers: How Sisterhood, Prayer, and Sex Changed a Nation at War* describes her experiences organizing for peace during Liberia's civil war; Gbowee and two other women received the 2011 Nobel Peace Prize for their efforts, which included bringing Christian and Muslim women together to advocate for peace.[9] Third, Nadia Bolz-Weber shares stories of how she has experienced God's amazing grace in her books *Pastrix: The Cranky, Beautiful Faith of a Sinner & Saint* and *Accidental Saints: Finding God in All the Wrong People*.[10] Each of these works gives elegant testimony to the ups and downs, struggles and joys of a life of faith, including what it means to be lifted up by God and to share God's love with others.

In conclusion, this book has aimed to show the breadth, depth, and riches of the Lutheran tradition, especially as presented in the *Book of Concord*. A church grounded in gospel freedom has options. Christians who experience faith as a lifelong journey with God will never be bored, run out of questions, or lack meaningful ways to live out their faith.

Far from being a closed legacy of the distant past, the *Book of Concord* continues to invite people to meet the Triune God in the scriptures and in worship, to take part in faith communities full of other simultaneous saints and sinners, and to care for this world in which God created us to serve as stewards and caretakers. Nearly five hundred years after Luther's "love and zeal for the truth" started a Reformation, this evangelical witness remains an exciting and fascinating way to enter adventures of faith yet in store.

---

8. Heidi Neumark, *Breathing Space: A Spiritual Journey in the South Bronx* (Boston: Beacon, 2004); and Heidi Neumark, *Hidden Inheritance: Family Secrets, Memory, and Faith* (Nashville: Abingdon, 2015).
9. Leymah Gbowee, *Mighty Be Our Powers: How Sisterhood, Prayer, and Sex Changed a Nation at War* (New York: Beast, 2011).
10. Nadia Bolz-Weber, *Pastrix: The Cranky, Beautiful Faith of a Sinner & Saint* (New York: Jericho, 2013); and Nadia Bolz-Weber, *Accidental Saints: Finding God in All the Wrong People* (New York: Convergent, 2015).

# Bibliography

Ahlstrom, Sidney. *A Religious History of the American People*, 2nd edition. New Haven: Yale University Press, 1972.

Altmann, Walter. *Luther and Liberation: A Latin American Perspective*. Translated by Mary Solberg. Minneapolis: Augsburg Fortress Press, 1992.

Arand, Charles. "Melanchthon's Rhetorical Argument for sola fide in the Apology," *Lutheran Quarterly* 14, 3 (Autumn 2000): 281–308.

Arand, Charles P., Robert Kolb, and James Nestingen. *The Lutheran Confessions: History and Theology of The Book of Concord*. Minneapolis: Fortress Press, 2012.

Augustine. *Augustine, Later Works*. Edited and translated by John Burnaby. Library of Christian Classics, Vol. 8. Philadelphia: Westminster, 1955.

____. *Confessions*. Translated by Henry Chadwick. Oxford: Oxford University Press, 1991.

*Die Bekenntnisschriften der evangelisch-lutherischen Kirche*. 11th edition. Göttingen: Vandenhoeck & Ruprecht, 1992.

Bolz-Weber, Nadia. *Accidental Saints: Finding God in All the Wrong People*. New York: Convergent, 2015.

____. *Pastrix: The Cranky, Beautiful Faith of a Sinner & Saint*. New York: Jericho, 2013.

Brecht, Martin. *Martin Luther*, 3 volumes. Translated by James Schaaf. Philadelphia and Minneapolis: Fortress Press, 1985–1993.

Bugenhagen, Johannes. *Selected Writings, Volumes 1 and 2*. Edited and translated by Kurt K. Hendel. Minneapolis: Fortress Press, 2015.

Calvin, John. *Institutes of the Christian Religion, Volumes 1 and 2*. Edited by John T. McNeil. Philadelphia: Westminster, 1960.

Denzinger, Heinrich and Adolf Schönmetzer, eds. *Enchiridion Symbolorum*, 33rd edition. Rome: Herder, 1965.

Dickens, A. G. *The English Reformation*, 2nd edition. University Park, PA: Pennsylvania State University Press, 1989.

Dingel, Irene and Günther Wartenberg, eds. *Politik und Bekenntnis: Die Reaktionen auf das Interim von 1548*. Leipzig: Evangelische Verlagsanstalt, 2006.

Edwards, Mark U. Jr., *Luther and the False Brethren*. Stanford: Stanford University Press, 1975.

_____. *Luther's Last Battles: Politics and Polemics, 1531-46*. Philadelphia: Fortress Press, 1983.

Gbowee, Leymah. *Mighty Be Our Powers: How Sisterhood, Prayer, and Sex Changed a Nation at War*. New York: Beast, 2011.

González, Justo. *The Story of Christianity, Volume 1: The Early Church to the Dawn of the Reformation*, revised and updated. New York: HarperCollins, 2010.

Grafton, David. *Piety, Politics, and Power: Lutherans Encountering Islam in the Middle East*. Eugene, OR: Pickwick, 2009.

Granquist, Mark. *Lutherans in America: A New History*. Minneapolis: Fortress Press, 2015.

Gregersen, Niels Henrik, Bo Holm, Ted Peters, and Peter Widmann, eds. *The Gift of Grace: The Future of Lutheran Theology*. Minneapolis: Fortress Press, 2005.

Gritsch, Eric. *A History of Lutheranism*. Minneapolis: Fortress Press, 2002.

Hall, Douglas John. *The Cross in Our Context: Jesus and the Suffering World*. Minneapolis: Fortress Press, 2003.

_____. *Lighten Our Darkness: Towards an Indigenous Theology of the Cross*, revised edition. Lima, OH: Academic Renewal Press, 2001.

Hamm, Berndt. *The Early Luther: Stages in a Reformation Reorientation*. Translated by Martin Lohrmann. Grand Rapids, MI: Eerdmans, 2014.

Hendrix, Scott. *Luther and the Papacy: Stages in a Reformation Conflict*. Philadelphia: Fortress Press, 1981.

_____. *Recultivating the Vineyard: The Reformation Agendas of Christianization*. Louisville: Westminster John Knox, 2004.

Hendrix, Scott and Timothy Wengert, editors. *Philip Melanchthon: Then and Now (1497-1997)*. Columbia, SC: Lutheran Theological Southern Seminary, 1999.

160

Ilić, Luka. *Theologian of Sin and Grace: The Process of Radicalization in the Theology of Matthias Flacius Illyricus.* Göttingen: Vandenhoek & Ruprecht, 2014.

Jacobson, Arland and James Aageson, editors. *The Future of Lutheranism in a Global Context.* Minneapolis: Augsburg Fortress Press, 2008.

Karant-Nunn, Susan and Merry Wiesner-Hanks. *Luther on Women: A Sourcebook.* Cambridge: Cambridge University Press, 2003.

Kiekegaard, Søren. *Fear and Trembling/Repetition.* Edited and translated by Howard Hong and Edna Hong. Princeton: Princeton University Press, 1983.

Kittelson, James. *Luther the Reformer: The Story of the Man and His Career.* Minneapolis: Augsburg, 1986.

Kolb, Robert. *Andreae and the Formula of Concord.* St. Louis: Concordia, 1977.

_____. *Confessing the Faith: Reformers Define the Church, 1530-1580.* St. Louis: Concordia, 1991.

_____, ed. *Lutheran Ecclesiastical Culture, 1550-1675.* Leiden: Brill, 2008.

Kolb, Robert and Timothy Wengert, eds. *The Book of Concord: The Confessions of the Evangelical Lutheran Church.* Minneapolis: Fortress Press, 2000.

Lagerquist, L. DeAne. *The Lutherans.* Westport, CT: Praeger, 1999.

Lathrop, Gordon and Timothy Wengert. *Christian Assembly: Marks of the Church in a Pluralistic Age.* Minneapolis: Fortress Press, 2004.

Lindberg, Carter. *Beyond Charity: Reformation Initiatives for the Poor.* Minneapolis: Fortress Press, 1993.

_____. *The European Reformations.* Malden, MA: Blackwell, 1996.

Lohrmann, Martin. *Bugenhagen's Jonah: Biblical Interpretation as Public Theology.* Minneapolis: Lutheran University Press, 2012.

Lorentzen, Tim. *Johannes Bugenhagen als Reformator der öffentlichen Fürsorge.* Tübingen: Mohr Siebeck, 2008.

Luther, Martin. *The Freedom of a Christian.* Translated by Mark Tranvik. Minneapolis: Fortress Press, 2008.

_____. *Luther's Works.* American edition. 55 volumes. Philadelphia: Fortress Press; St. Louis: Concordia, 1955–1986.

_____. *Martin Luther's Christmas Book.* Edited by Roland Bainton. Philadelphia: Westminster, 1948.

MacCulloch, Diarmaid. *The Reformation.* New York: Viking, 2003.

Marty, Martin. *Martin Luther.* New York: Penguin, 2004.

161

McKim, Donald, ed. *The Cambridge Companion to Martin Luther*. Cambridge: Cambridge University Press, 2003.

Melanchthon, Philip. "Loci Communes Theologici." In *Melanchthon and Bucer*, edited by Wilhelm Pauck. Translated by Lowell J. Satre, 3–154. Philadelphia: Westminster, 1969.

Neumark, Heidi. *Breathing Space: A Spiritual Journey in the South Bronx*. Boston: Beacon, 2004.

____. *Hidden Inheritance: Family Secrets, Memory, and Faith*. Nashville: Abingdon, 2015.

Oberman, Heiko. *The Harvest of Medieval Theology*. Cambridge, MA: Harvard University Press, 1963.

____. *Luther: Man between God and the Devil*. Translated by Eileen Walliser-Schwarzbart. New Haven: Yale University Press, 1989.

____. *The Roots of Anti-Semitism in the Age of Renaissance and Reformation*. Translated by James I. Porter. Philadelphia: Fortress Press, 1984.

Pelikan, Jaroslav. *Luther the Expositor*. St. Louis: Concordia, 1959.

Peters, Albrecht. *Commentary on Luther's Catechisms: Lord's Prayer*. Translated by Daniel Thies. St. Louis: Concordia, 2011.

Plato, *Great Dialogues of Plato*. Translated by W. H. D. Rouse. New York: Penguin, 1984.

Posset, Franz. *Unser Martin: Martin Luther aus der Sicht katholischer Sympathizanten*. Münster: Aschendorff, 2015.

Rajashekar, Paul. *Luther and Islam: An Asian Perspective*. Göttingen: Vandenhoeck & Ruprecht, 1990.

Reed, Luther D. *The Lutheran Liturgy*. Philadelphia: Muhlenberg, 1947.

Russell, William R. *Luther's Theological Testament: The Schmalkald Articles*. Minneapolis: Fortress Press, 1995.

____. "The Smalcald Articles: Luther's Theological Testament." *Lutheran Quarterly* 5, 3 (Autumn 1991), 277–96.

Scheible, Heinz. "Fifty Years of Melanchthon Research." *Lutheran Quarterly* 26, 2 (Summer 2012): 164–80.

Schramm, Brooks and Kirsi Stjerna. *Martin Luther, the Bible, and the Jewish People: A Reader*. Minneapolis: Fortress, 2012.

Schütz Zell, Katharina. *Church Mother: The Writings of a Protestant Reformation in Sixteenth-Century Germany*. Edited by Elsie McKee. Chicago: Chicago University Press, 2006.

Sider, Ronald, ed. *Karlstadt's Battle with Luther: Documents in a Liberal-Radical Debate*. Philadelphia: Fortress Press, 1978.

Stolt, Birgit. "Luther's Translation of the Bible." *Lutheran Quarterly* 28, 4 (Winter 2014): 373–74.

Stjerna, Kirsi. *Women and the Reformation*. Malden, MA: Blackwell, 2008.

Stout, Jeffrey. *Democracy and Tradition*. Princeton: Princeton University Press, 2004.

Stupperich, Robert. *Melanchthon*. Translated by Robert Fischer. Philadelphia: Westminster,1965.

Volz, Hans, ed. *Urkunden und Aketenstücke zur Geschichte von Martin Luthers Schmalkaldischen Artikeln (1536-1574)*. Berlin: de Gruyter, 1957.

Wengert, Timothy. *A Formula for Parish Practice: Using the Formula of Concord in Congregations*. Grand Rapids, MI: Eerdmans, 2006.

_____. *Human Freedom, Christian Righteousness*. Oxford: Oxford University Press, 1998.

_____. *Martin Luther's Catechisms: Forming the Faith*. Minneapolis: Fortress Press, 2009.

_____. *Philip Melanchthon, Speaker of the Reformation: Wittenberg's Other Reformer*. Burlington, VT: Ashgate, 2010.

_____. *Priesthood, Pastors, Bishops: Public Ministry for the Reformation and Today*. Minneapolis: Fortress Press, 2008.

Wiesner-Hanks, Merry. *Women and Gender in Early Modern Europe*. Cambridge: Cambridge University Press, 2008.

# Index of Names and Subjects

# Index of Scripture